TUSCANY

Jack Altman

JPMGUIDES

Contents

Fold-out map

Tuscany

Florence

This Way Tuscany

Culture and Good Living

It's all here. A tour of Tuscany will reveal everything that the popular image of Italy may conjure up: the grandest of Renaissance painting and sculpture; architectural masterpieces in its palazzi, villas and churches; enchanting landscapes of olive groves, vineyards and rows of lofty cypresses marching up to hilltop villages; a glass of Chianti and plate of steaming pasta on a piazza terrace. There's sea and sand, too, on the long Mediterranean coast, and for those who want to cool off, the lovely Alpine highlands in the north.

Hills cover two-thirds of the territory. The highest point is the peak of Mount Pisanino, 1,945 m (6,379 ft), northeast of Carrara. The valleys of the Chianti vineyards and the Arno river, and the Maremma marshlands southwest of Siena comprise the lowlands. The Arno, brown with silt, flows 241 km (150 miles) from Mount Falterona, northeast of Florence, down to the Mediterranean beyond Pisa.

The good things of Tuscan life extend beyond the finery of Florence's luxury boutiques. Siena, Pistoia and Sansepolcro are renowned for embroidered fabrics, Arezzo and Chiusi for ceramics, Pisa and Volterra for alabaster. Gourmets go not only for the finest Chianti Classico, but also the wines of Montepulciano and Montalcino.

Eternal Loggerheads

Despite the distinctive character of its culture within the Italian nation, Tuscany presents a regional unity only to the outside world. Harmony remains an ideal of its Renaissance art rather than a fact of its daily life. Inside its borders, Tuscany is split into dozens of rivalries between the adjacent communes of its townships. This has been true ever since the ancient Etruscans were conquered by Rome because their 12 major towns could not form a solid defensive alliance. The medieval wars of Siena and Florence are gone, but not forgotten. You only have to consider the difficulty of public transport between villages of the Florentine region and those around Siena—the bus networks are not compatible. Old trading rivals Pisa and Lucca still engage in municipal squabbles. The people of Massa are reluctant to show visitors the route to the marble quarries of the neighbouring town of Carrara.

Local pride is at its fiercest inside the city limits. San Gimignano's celebrated "medieval Manhattan" towers are relics of merchant dynasties each trying to prove its superiority. The passions aroused by Siena's Palio horse race are stoked by the year-round rivalries of the town's 17 districts. Neighbourhoods in other towns let off steam cheering—and betting—on the barrel-rollers in Montepulciano, the jousters in Arezzo's Giostra del Saraceno or toughs trying to push each other across the bridge in Pisa's Gioco del Ponte.

The people carry within themselves another perennial contradiction: they declare themselves Catholic and vote in most towns for Communist mayors—or at least, since the 1990s, their more democratic but still decidedly leftist successors.

Light and Colour

For all the conflicts, nobody would deny the serene influence of the play of light and colour on the landscape and on the painters, sculptors and architects who grew up in the region. Though many artists gravitated to the main centre of political power in Florence, other Tuscan cities could boast their own home-grown talent and genius.

The jewel-like delicacy of the cathedral, baptistery and almost miraculous Leaning Tower in Pisa set the tone for medieval Italian architecture. The Pisano family took its sculptural talents all over Tuscany. Siena's taste for warm colour and elegance created a school of painters—Duccio di Buoninsegna, Simone Martini, the Lorenzetti brothers and Sassetta—quite distinct from their cooler Florentine counterparts. A master apart from his 15th-century contemporaries, Piero della Francesca produced his greatest art in Arezzo and the surrounding towns of eastern Tuscany. And the joy of seeing these artistic masterpieces—in Sansepolcro, Massa Marittima, Lucca or Volterra—is to come across them in the setting of their inspiration, that most glorious creation of man and nature, the Tuscan landscape. Paint your own picture.

Triangular Bonus

A weekend excursion outside Tuscany's southern border takes you to the green and pleasant region of Umbria. Visit there a triangle of towns—the hilltop tranquillity of Gubbio, with its splendid ceramics; the lively university town of Perugia and the works of Perugino, its best-loved artist; and the pilgrimage town of St Francis's Assisi, rising like a great ship out of the flat landscape.

Etruscan Beginnings

The brilliant but mysterious Etruscans flourished from the 10th to 4th centuries BC. "Mysterious" because of their origins: historians have not yet agreed whether they were indigenous to Italy or settlers from the eastern Mediterranean or elsewhere. From predecessors known as Villanovans, migrants from Central Europe, they had learned to smelt iron from Elba and Arezzo and use the copper mined from the Tuscan hills. They refined Etruscan culture through contact and trade with the Phoenicians and Greeks, and enjoyed a comfortable life farming wheat, olives and abundant fruit.

Their principal towns included Volterra, Fiesole, Arezzo, Cortona and Chiusi. At their height, in the 7th century BC, Etruscan communities extended south through Rome down to Capua and Salerno. Rather than form a united nation, the towns preferred a loose confederation of autonomous monarchies, and gathered together only for religious festivals. Imperial expansion did not seem to interest them, and their only aggressive behaviour was a little piracy on the high seas to bring in a few extra luxuries.

It was the lack of political unity and their taste for the comfortable life that brought about the Etruscans' downfall. They proved no match for tough Gallic invaders from the north. In the 4th century BC, Rome broke with the weakened confederation and began its rise to empire. Among Etruscan cities, only Volterra resisted, finally yielding in 90 BC.

Romans Come and Go

If the Romans did not appreciate the way of life of the fun-loving Etruscans, they did value the strategic hilltop positions of their towns. They reinforced the defences of Cortona, Fiesole and Volterra. Under Augustus, a sleepy little farming community dependent on Volterra grew into the major military base of Siena. Other towns sprang up in the plain, notably the Pistoia garrison astride the new Via Cassia highway and a port on the Arno river at Florence. At the mouth of the Arno—and junction of Via Cassia and the Via Aurelia coast road to Gaul—the commercial port of Pisa, originally a Greek settlement, became a naval base for the Roman fleet. Neighbouring Lucca controlled the Alpine trade route to northern Europe. Arezzo supplied iron for the empire's munitions and, from surrounding farmland, grain for the hungry capital.

By the 5th century AD, after the empire had crumbled, Visigoth, Hun and Ostrogoth invasions left little trace of Roman rule in Tuscany—mostly remains of amphitheatres in Arezzo, Fiesole and Lucca, where brick arches form part of houses around the Piazza del Mercato.

Arrival of the Communes

Lombards—"Long Beards" originally from north Germany—seized Tuscany in the 6th century and ruled for over 200 years. A duchy at Lucca administered the territory for the Lombard court, which was based in Pavia, south of Milan. The merchants of Lucca, ever pragmatic, switched their allegiance to Charlemagne's Frankish empire in 774. They expanded their Mediterranean trade after their fleet took Corsica and Sardinia from the Arabs in the 9th century. Thereafter, other Tuscan cities—Pisa, Siena, Pistoia, Florence—followed Lucca's example in pursuing their own goals by playing off feudal allegiances to the pope or the Holy Roman Emperor in their contest for control of Italy. The cities concentrated on forming strong communes to administer their lands and overseas interests. They happily sided with the pope's forces known as Guelphs or the emperor's Ghibellines, depending on who was making the best offer at the time.

THE GOOD THINGS

In the best latterday Italian tradition, the Etruscans preferred the good things of life to fighting wars. They traded their iron and copper for gold and silver with which they crafted exquisite jewellery—and inlays for their teeth. They pioneered the chariot in Italy, not as a vehicle of war but for racing at their hippodromes. They gambled and danced, and used music to accompany their every activity—boxing, baking bread or beating a recalcitrant slave. They tried to win over their Gallic invaders by showing them how to make wine from grapes. Their prudish Roman conquerors berated them for making love in public. Worst of all, in the eyes of Greeks and Romans alike, Etruscan women enjoyed entirely too much freedom. They disposed of their own property, dared to beat their men at table games, and even sat down to dinner, as one writer complained, not only with their husbands but with any other husband who might be available.

Battles continued throughout the Middle Ages, mirroring the local rivalries that have continued to this day. The history of Tuscany became that of its most powerful communes.

Pisa and Lucca: Neighbours and Rivals

From the Middle Ages until the 15th century, Pisa and Lucca each enjoyed a heyday of spectacular prosperity. As Tuscany's major seaport since antiquity, Pisa matched Venice and Genoa with its medieval maritime empire of trading posts, extending from Corsica, Sardinia and Sicily east to Egypt, Palestine and Syria.

The wealth accumulated by commerce and piracy helped to build the magnificent cathedral with its baptistery and campanile. The earth for the monumental Camposanto cemetery was transported from the Holy Land on Pisan ships that participated in the Crusades. The city's building boom gave new life to the marble quarries of Carrara, which had been abandoned since Roman times. The luminous white edifices set the style for Romanesque churches throughout Italy, reflecting the decorative influence of Pisa's contacts with the eastern Mediterranean. The sculptor-architects Nicola and Andrea Pisano found more work in Siena, Florence, Pistoia and Orvieto.

Pisa's commercial empire was brought to an end in 1284 when Genoa defeated its navy. The city foundered as nobles and merchants fought over the remaining spoils. As factions sought outside support from Guelphs or Ghibellines, Pisa was subjected to a series of foreign rulers until it reluctantly accepted Florentine protection in 1406. Civil peace permitted the university to revive and, at the end of the 16th century, attracted Galileo back to his home town to teach mathematics.

Without a seaport outlet to the Mediterranean, Lucca, in contrast to Pisa, amassed a fortune on inland routes across the Alps to northern and eastern Europe. Its skilful bankers made profitable loans to Europe's kings and princes, and uncompromising silk merchants struck tough bargains in Poland, Hungary, Germany and France. Thus did the moneymen finance Lucca's handsome churches and palazzi—and save them from destruction by northern invaders by paying off the armies to bypass the city on their way south. In Tuscany at the start of the 14th century, the city's prosperity was second only to that of Florence.

Then, Lucca, too, was ripped apart by bloody battles between Guelphs and Ghibellines. Genoa, Parma, Verona, even arch-enemy Pisa, each made assaults on the town's autonomy. Finally, rather than accept the supreme insult of subjection to Florence, Lucca preferred to throw in its lot with German emperor Charles IV. He guaranteed its status as a republic independent of any Italian power.

Siena:
From Bankers to Saints

Its emblem of Senius and Aschius suckled by a she-wolf shows that Siena was founded by pagan Rome. But it always had a special relationship with Christian Rome, too. With the pope's blessing, Siena's bishop wielded both civic and ecclesiastical control of the city until the 12th century when nobles led a popular revolt. The ensuing struggle pitched workers against merchants, merchants against nobles, while the church sided in turn with all three factions.

As a matter of principle, Siena stood against whatever its great rival Florence was for. It usually supported the Ghibellines against the papal Guelphs. Except when one of the city's own sons, Rolando Bandinelli, became Pope Alexander III in 1159. Siena money financed the pope's victorious struggle against Emperor Friedrich Barbarossa. In 1179, Alexander III returned triumphantly to his home town to consecrate the new cathedral.

Through its close papal ties, Siena's bankers acquired a pious weapon with which to gouge exorbitant interest payments from reluctant Catholic debtors. The pope, as "collateral" for his own loans, signed letters of excommunication naming bad debtors and damning them to hell—until the debt was paid in full.

By the 13th century, Siena had extended its financial influence throughout Europe, becoming for a time wealthier and more popu-

---

GUELPHS AND GHIBELLINES

Guelpho comes from Welf, a Bavarian dynasty supporting the pope; *Ghibellino* from the Swabian family of Waiblingen, which supported the emperor. Ghibelline forces built swallowtail blocks on their battlements to distinguish their defences from the square battlements of the Guelphs. More meaningful distinctions are hard to find. Within one town, factions would side with one or the other party—often, but not always, conservatives with the Guelphs and progressives with the Ghibellines. Modern historians note that traditionally Guelph towns have often supported Christian Democrats and other right-wing parties, while Ghibellines have gone to the Communists or their reformed successors, the PDS.

lous than Paris or London. The ongoing fight with Florence for control of central Italy proved its downfall. It had recovered from defeat in 1207 to score a splendid but short-lived victory over Florentine forces at Montaperti in 1260. The papacy sided with ever-faithful Florence, pronouncing anathema on the whole city of Siena which, after Alexander III's death, had switched allegiance back to the Ghibellines. Florence in turn ruthlessly routed Sienese forces at Colle di Val d'Elsa, prompting Siena's merchants and bankers to turn Guelph, in submission to Florence's now overwhelming power.

A brief respite enabled the town to complete its formidable Palazzo Pubblico and add a grand façade to the cathedral. Then fierce factional conflicts resumed. Banks collapsed, and the Black Death of 1348 devastated the population. In adversity, saints replaced bankers in influencing the papacy. Catherine (Siena-born Caterina Benincasa, 1347–80) and Bernardino (born in Massa, 1380–1444) both set a fervent spiritual example for the church. From the 15th century, foreign rulers took over, and lands were sold to the Medici of Florence. As a sleepy backwater, Siena could at least keep its magnificent medieval monuments intact.

From the Medici to Modern Times

Once Florence asserted its supremacy in the 15th century, largely through the power of the Medici dynasty, the rest of Tuscany took a political back seat. It provided a battleground for the city's struggles with its enemies, such as the Duke of Urbino's army marching up the Chianti valley in 1479. In order to withstand other assaults, Cosimo I de' Medici, Duke of Tuscany (1537–74), and his successors built a network of fortresses extending from Florence to Siena, Arezzo, Livorno and the island of Elba. Lucca, still independent, defiantly set up its own fortifications. With Pisa's harbour silting up, the duchy developed Livorno (Leghorn to the English) as its major seaport, and built a new canal to link it to the Arno river. Malarial marshlands were drained and converted to farmland in the Maremma southwest of Siena, the plains around Pisa, and the Valdichiana south of Arezzo.

The cultural contribution remained noteworthy. Siena continued to produce fine painters such as Sassetta, Beccafumi and Sodoma. Sansepolcro in Arezzo's hinterland produced the unique genius of Piero della Francesca. Pius II had architect Bernardo Rossellino transform the Pope's home town of Corsignano into

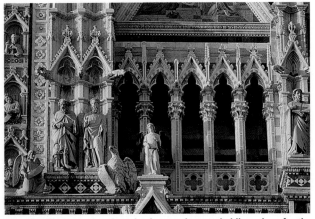

Giovanni Pisano sculpted patriarchs, prophets and philosophers for the façade of Siena's cathedral.

the "ideal city" of Pienza, a model of Renaissance urban planning. Humanist scholar and classical linguist Angelo Poliziano took his name from his home town, Montepulciano, as did Arezzo's brilliantly bawdy poet Pietro Aretino. Galileo travelled from Pisa to teach in Siena, Padua and Florence and become the duke's court mathematician.

In the 17th and 18th centuries, Tuscany became just a pawn in the European power struggles of Austria, Spain and France. The Medici court retired to the region's vineyards and country villas. Having created the short-lived kingdom of Etruria, Napoleon Bonaparte spent a brief exile on Elba in 1814 before his last hurrah at Waterloo. His sister Pauline went off to Viareggio and turned it into the smartest resort on the Riviera. In the 1840s, a railway line built by Scottish engineer Robert Stephenson linked Florence to the coast via Pistoia, Pisa and Livorno. Strategically vital Livorno later attracted heavy World War II bombardment.

At the end of the 20th century, Pisa was the focus of two symbolically important events. In 1992, Galileo was rehabilitated by the Vatican. Two years later, scientists and engineers halted the decline of the Leaning Tower. 11

On the Scene

Florence is a city to be savoured, its finest monuments and works of art to be lingered over. The surrounding region is equally rich. The popular Chianti wine country takes in excursions to historic Fiesole, San Gimignano and Volterra. The Siena region runs south through Pienza, with more fine wines at Montalcino and Montepulciano. Northern Tuscany centres on monumental Pisa and Lucca. The South Coast includes a trip out to the island of Elba and extends inland to Massa Marittima. Arezzo's region covers the culturally rich but little explored hinterland of eastern Tuscany. And over the border in Umbria, explore the magic triangle of Perugia, Gubbio and Assisi.

◆ FLORENCE

Piazza del Duomo, Piazza della Signoria, Uffizi, San Lorenzo to San Marco, Mercato Nuovo to Santa Maria Novella, Bargello to Santa Croce, South of the Arno, Fiesole

Few nations, let alone cities, can boast such an overpowering array of talent concentrated over so short a period of time. The names of some of Florence's greatest sons—Boccaccio, Botticelli, Cellini, Dante, Donatello, Giotto, Leonardo da Vinci, Michelangelo, Machiavelli—are known the world over. Not bad for a city whose great period spanned less than 300 years.

In the narrow streets loom the massive stone palazzi with names straight out of history, like Strozzi, Pazzi, Salviati, and above all the Medici.

Piazza del Duomo

The historic centre of Florence is compact enough to explore easily on foot. Around the Piazza del Duomo are some of the busiest shopping streets in the city.

Ghiberti's Doors of Paradise; a labour of love that took 25 years.

13

Duomo

The great cathedral, in the form of a Latin cross, takes up most of the space, its bright marble—white from Carrara, green from Prato, pink from Maremma—startling in contrast to the sombre ochres and greys of the surrounding buildings. Work on the cathedral was begun by Arnolfo di Cambio (1296) and continued after his death by Giotto, Francesco Talenti and others. The huge dome, built in 1436, was designed by Filippo Brunelleschi, and with its vast proportions—48 m (157 ft) in diameter and 55 m (180 ft) high—is an architectural masterpiece.

The three airy aisles emphasize the echoing immensity of the interior. On the inner façade is a clock painted with four heads of the Prophets by Paolo Uccello in 1443, and to the left of the entrance, a painting by Domenico di Michelino, *Evocation of Dante*. Below the high altar is a bronze shrine by Lorenzo Ghiberti containing relics of Saint Zanobius, one of the first bishops of Florence. Ghiberti also designed the round windows. The fresco inside the dome, depicting the *Last Judgment*, was painted by Vasari and Zuccari, and finished in 1579.

Campanile di Giotto

Standing apart from the Duomo, the elegant bell-tower was designed by Giotto, who began its construction in 1334. He died three years later, and his pupil Andrea Pisano took over. The last three floors were finished by Francesco Talenti. The change of style is clearly visible at each stage, as each architect added his personal touch. The tower is 85 m (280 ft) high. Climb the 416 steps winding up to the top, to enjoy a superb panorama.

Baptistery

Dating from the 4th and 5th centuries, the octagonal baptistery is the most ancient building in Florence. It's fascinating to sit on the cathedral steps and watch people studying the three magnificent doors of gilded bronze, which trace the evolution of Florentine sculpture from Gothic to Renaissance. The south doors (1328–38) are the work of Andrea of Pisano, a pupil of Giotto. Lorenzo Ghiberti began work on the north doors in 1403; the panels recount the life of Christ. His work so pleased the Florentines that he was commissioned for the east doors in 1425. It took him more than 25 years to complete this work, whose ten large square panels illustrate scenes from the Old Testament, including the creation of Adam and Eve, Noah's ark and Moses receiving the Ten Commandments. Michelangelo was so impressed, he called them the "Doors of Paradise".

Inside, the walls are covered in marble, and the beautiful cupola is covered in scintillating mosaics by several artists including Cimabue, Coppo and Giotto. An octagon indicates the spot where children used to be baptised on New Year's Eve.

Museo dell'Opera del Duomo

If the Duomo and baptistery seem cavernous and empty, that's because all their treasures have been transferred to this museum, opened in 1891. Here you can see choir lofts sculpted by Luca della Robbia and Donatello, works by Ghiberti, Pollaiuolo and Michelangelo, including the *Pietà* he intended for his tomb. Also on display are the tools used by Brunelleschi to construct the dome,

his wooden models of the dome and lantern—and his death mask. Michelangelo sculpted his statue of *David* in the courtyard, now covered with glass.

Casa di Dante Alighieri

The author of the epic poem *Divine Comedy*, Dante Alighieri, haunts the narrow streets just south of the cathedral. This house reconstructed between 1875 and 1910 is said to be his birthplace, though there's nothing to prove it and the original building has disappeared. A small museum recounts his life and work.

Piazza della Signoria

If the Piazza del Duomo is Florence's religious heart, its political centre lies in the Piazza della Signoria. On the south side is the Loggia della Signoria (or dei Lanzi), built in the late 14th century and now sheltering several statues, including two works by Giambologna and a magnificent bronze *Perseus* by Cellini. The roof of the loggia is the terrace of the Uffizi's café.

In front of the Palazzo Vecchio stands a copy of Michelangelo's *David* and a 16th-century marble group of *Hercules and Cacus* by Baccio Bandinelli. The statue of Neptune surmounting the fountain (Fontana del Nettuno) is the work of Bartolomeo Ammannati, between 1560 and 1575. The 15 water-nymphs at the sea-god's feet are by Giambologna, who also sculpted the nearby equestrian statue of Cosimo I.

Palazzo Vecchio

Built between 1298 and 1314 to plans drawn by Arnolfo di Cambio, the fortress-like Old Palace is the very symbol of the city. Initially the seat of the supreme magistrature (Signoria) in 1293, it changed its function several times. It was renamed the Palazzo Vecchio when the Medici family moved across the river to the Palazzo Pitti.

An impressive staircase by Vasari leads to the Salone dei Cinquecento (1495) where meetings of the city council were held, and where the first parliament of a united Italy met. The walls and ceiling are covered in frescoes by Vasari, and there's an exceptional statue of *Victory* by Michelangelo. Do not miss the delightful Studiolo di Francesco I, a study designed by Vasari and covered with painted panels representing the four elements, Earth, Water, Fire and Air. The highlight is the 15th-century Sala dei Gigli (Hall of the Lilies), decorated with heraldry, a gilt-panelled ceiling and frescoes by Ghirlandaio. The original of Donatello's bronze *Judith and Holofernes* also stands here; the one in the piazza outside is a copy.

Uffizi

To the right of the Palazzo Vecchio, the galleries of the Uffizi stretch all the way to the Arno. Built as headquarters for government offices (hence the name), this is now one of the world's most famous art museums and contains Italy's finest collection of paintings covering the cream of Italian and European art from the 13th to the 18th centuries. Start with the altarpieces of those early Tuscan "greats", Cimabue and Giotto, then enjoy Fra Angelico's *Coronation of the Virgin*, full of light and music, and Paolo Uccello's *Battle of San Romano*, an astounding exercise in perspective and volume. Best-loved among Renaissance paintings are Botticelli's *Birth of Venus* and *Primavera* (Spring). Of the 15th-century Flemish paintings, Hugo van der Goes' huge triptych of the *Adoration of the Shepherds* is outstanding.

One room belongs to Leonardo da Vinci, featuring the Baptism of Christ, painted with his teacher, Verrocchio. The exquisite *Annunciation* is entirely Leonardo's work. There is but one work by the great Michelangelo in the museum: his earliest known painting (1503), the round panel of the *Holy Family*.

Among German masterpieces in the Uffizi, don't miss Dürer's *Portrait of His Father* and the

From David *to* Cosimo I, *Piazza della Signoria puts Florentine sculpture in perspective.*

Adoration of the Magi; and Cranach's lifelike portraits of Luther, his renegade-nun wife and a solidly Germanic Adam and Eve.

San Lorenzo to San Marco

Between church and monastery spreads the University district, full of fascinating shops and friendly neighbourhood bars and cafés.

Church of San Lorenzo

Begun in 1419, this Renaissance church is the collective work of the great artists of the city's Golden Age. It contains numerous masterpieces including a marble tabernacle of 1460 and two bronze pulpits by Donatello. The Old Sacristy is the work of Brunelleschi and Donatello.

The New Sacristy (access from Piazza Madonna degli Aldobrandini) was Michelangelo's first architectural work: note the sculptures on the sarcophagi and the statues of Lorenzo and Giuliano de' Medici. The Medici family ceremonies were celebrated in this church: their tombs are contained in the Cappelle Medicee (access from Piazza Madonna degli Aldobrandini). The Cappella dei Principi (Chapel of the Princes), sumptuously clad in rare marbles and mosaics of precious stones, is not to be missed.

17

Biblioteca Laurenziana

This celebrated library was designed by Michelangelo to house the collections of manuscripts acquired by Cosimo the Elder and his sons Piero and Lorenzo. The monumental staircase, begun by Michelangelo, was completed by Vasari and Ammannati.

Markets

The San Lorenzo market, the biggest and most popular in Florence, clusters around the church and spreads along nearby streets. It's a good place to find a bargain pair of shoes. To the north, the monumental covered Mercato Centrale (1870–74) was designed by a Milanese architect, Giuseppe Mengoni, and combines brick and glass in a framework of cast iron. The stalls are devoted entirely to food.

Galleria dell'Accademia di Belle Arti

In 1873, having weathered almost four centuries in front of the Palazzo della Signoria, Michelangelo's *David* found a home here in the Academy of Fine Arts on Via Ricasoli. The world-famous statue was sculpted in 1501 when the artist was 25. The rooms are full of sculpture and paintings from the 13th to the 18th centuries. Note Michelangelo's unfinished *Four Slaves*, who look as though they are struggling to escape from their mantle of rough marble.

San Marco

Comprising church, convent and cloisters, this complex dating from 1299 is grouped behind a baroque façade overlooking a busy square. The convent is now one of Florence's most interesting museums, containing many paintings and frescoes by Fra Angelico, who lived here as a monk.

In the Pilgrim's Hospice, you can see some fine retables and altar paintings, and an enchanting wooden panel originally intended as a cupboard door, with 35 small paintings including an *Annunciation* where the Angel Gabriel has wings striped in red, blue and yellow. Beyond the frescoed cloister, the Small Refectory is decorated with a mural by Ghirlandaio of *The Last Supper*.

In the upstairs dormitory, each of the monks' cells is adorned with a fresco by Fra Angelico or his pupils. At the head of the stairs is the luminous *Angel of the Annunciation*, bowing slightly. In some of the cells, part of the floor has been removed so you can see ancient paintings underneath. At the end of the cells to the right of the stairs is Cosimo de' Medici's "duplex", where he came to meditate, and at the far end are Girolamo Savonarola's quarters, with his desk and black hooded cloak.

Mercato Nuovo to Santa Maria Novella

This is largely a commercial area, dominated by the main railway station, nearby bus station and chaotic traffic. Amid the big buildings, however, are some gems worth seeking out.

Mercato Nuovo

Beneath a Renaissance loggia, built in the mid-16th century to shelter goldsmiths and silk merchants, the New Market is famous for its Florentine straw articles. But you'll also see racks of leather jackets, bags and shoes and ceramics.

Look for the famous Fontana del Porcellino (1612): the "little pig" is in fact a wild boar. Rub his nose and throw a coin in the fountain and you will soon come back to Florence.

Santa Maria Novella

Make your way down Via de' Tornabuoni past the 15th-century Palazzo Strozzi, one of the most beautiful private residences in the whole of the city, to the great monastic church, Santa Maria Novella. The façade, by Leon Battista Alberti, is entirely covered in inlaid marble. Inside, the three aisles were rebuilt by Vasari in 1565. There are several important works such as Masaccio's *Holy Trinity* of 1427 (left aisle), frescoes by Ghirlandaio in the Tornabuoni Chapel *(Apparition of the Angel to Zachariah in the Temple)*, a marble pulpit by Brunelleschi.

Chiostri Monumentali

At the exit of Santa Maria Novella, a baroque gateway leads to the cloisters of the ancient monastery, a haven of peace. The Chiostro Verde (Green Cloister) is so called because of the dominant colour of Paolo Uccello's frescoes, *The Flood* and the *Story of Noah*. The Cappellone degli Spagnoli (Chapel of the Spaniards), a building by Talenti, was the old chapterhouse of the monastery.

Bargello to Santa Croce

The area around Santa Croce still has a medieval feel to it, especially in the narrow streets around Borgo dei Greci and Via Torta. You'll discover antique dealers and carpenter's workshops, and near the Teatro Verdi, on the site of the former prison (Stinche), Florence's most famous *gelateria*. The Medicis used to stage jousts on the huge Piazza Santa Croce, lined on one side with a row of buildings with a cantilevered and frescoed upper storey.

Museo Nazionale del Bargello

This imposing medieval fortress, dating from the 13th–14th centuries, was the city's first town

19

Medieval Ponte Vecchio, built on the site of a Roman bridge at the Arno's narrowest point.

hall. It became the seat of the magistrates responsible for law and order—whose coats of arms adorn the courtyard—and in the 16th century housed the offices of the chief of police, or Bargello. The building also served a spell as a prison in the 18th century. It now contains one of the world's finest sculpture collections, with works by Michelangelo, Cellini, Sansovino and Giambologna as well as Donatello's bronze *David*, the first nude statue of the Renaissance, and Verrocchio's *David*, with the head of Goliath between his feet. There are also several small collections, as charming as they are varied: Re-

naissance jewellery, Venetian glass, ivories, majolica and small bronzes.

Casa Buonarroti
Michelangelo drew the plans for this small palace, which he then had constructed on a plot of land purchased in 1508. At Via Ghibellina 70, it is now a museum displaying his drawings, letters and portraits, and a collection of 17th-century paintings illustrating the main events of his life.

Santa Croce
The largest Franciscan church in the city was designed by Arnolfo in 1294, and it took 100 years to

build. The immense Gothic nave contains the tombs of many celebrated Italians including Michelangelo (inside the door to the right), designed by Vasari. The tomb of Dante Alighieri is empty, for his body remained in Ravenna. Galileo, Machiavelli and Ghiberti are also entombed here. The nineteen chapels harbour numerous treasures and have beautiful stained-glass windows. To the right of the altar, the Bardi Chapel and neighbouring Peruzzi Chapel are decorated with frescoes by Giotto, the first illustrating the life of St Francis, and the second that of St John.

Museo di Santa Croce

The church museum, in the cloisters, houses works by the great Florentine masters such as Donatello, Bronzino and others. The famous *Crucifix* by Cimabue, seriously damaged in the floods of 1966 is here, meticulously restored, as well as Andrea Orcagna's frescoes of the *Last Judgment*. Outside stands a memorial to Florence Nightingale.

South of the Arno

Cross over the river by the Ponte Vecchio. When you have explored the Pitti Palace and rested a while in the Boboli Gardens, walk along the river bank and up to Piazzale Michelangelo, for a painterly view of the city. From here you can catch the bus no. 13 which will sweep you through the hills and back to the city centre.

Ponte Vecchio

Spanning the Arno at its narrowest point, Florence's oldest and most picturesque bridge has been destroyed several times by floods but it was spared in 1944 when all the other bridges were blown up by the Germans. Today's construction dates from 1345. Originally the shops were occupied by fishmongers, butchers and tanners, who swept their waste into the river. In 1594 Duke Ferdinand did away with this smelly commerce and replaced the traders with jewellers and goldsmiths, many of whom built extensions over the parapet. Downstream, you can see the elegant Santa Trinita bridge, originally built in 1257.

Palazzo Pitti

This is the largest of the Florentine palaces. Begun in 1457 by Brunelleschi on the orders of Luca Pitti, a banker and rival of the Medici, the palace was inherited by Eleonora di Toledo, wife of Cosimo I de' Medici. King Vittorio Emanuele II of the House of Savoy lived here in 1860 when Florence enjoyed a brief period as capital of Italy. Today the palace comprises numerous magnificent museums: the Royal Apartments 21 of the House of Savoy; a gallery of modern art; the Palatine gallery; the silver museum; and more.

Giardino di Boboli

This delightful, slightly dishevelled park laid out behind the palace over a hillside is full of birds, fountains, and long avenues of shady trees with hundreds of marble statues of angels, gods and mythical creatures half-hidden behind bushes. The first plans were drawn up around 1550 by a pupil of Michelangelo, Niccolò Pericoli, known as Tribolo.

At the top of the hill, above the amphitheatre, is the Casino del Cavaliere, housing the Porcelain Museum. Turning right after the amphitheatre, follow the avenue of cypresses all the way to the Isolotto, an ornamental pond with the Fountain of the Oceans in the centre, surrounded by greenery. To the left of the amphitheatre is the Kaffeehaus, overlooking the city, and further on a strange grotto designed by Buontalenti. Nearby, the Fountain of Bacchus depicts Cosimo I's favourite jester Morgante, astride a turtle.

Piazzale Michelangelo

You can climb the steps from Piazza G. Poggi or take bus 12 or 13 up winding Viale Michelangelo to reach this wide terrace, to enjoy the view of Florence and the surrounding hills. In the centre stands the monument to Michelangelo, with a bronze reproduction of *David* and four of the Medici Chapel statues.

San Salvatore al Monte

This church was a favourite of Michelangelo, who called it "la bella villanella", the beautiful country girl. Construction (1499–1504) was by Simone del Pollaiuolo, financed by the Guild of Calimala, whose business was the refining and dyeing of cloth and the importation of exotic goods. The sign of this guild, the eagle, can be seen on the left side of the church.

San Miniato al Monte

St Minias, an early Christian martyred in the 3rd century under Decius, is said to have carried his severed head to the top of the highest hill south of Florence, and set it down on the site where this church was built in 1013. With its green and white marble façade, it is a fine example of Florentine Romanesque architecture. The marble-encrusted floor depicting the signs of the zodiac looks like delicate lacework.

The bell tower was built in the 16th century. During the siege of Florence, Michelangelo protected it from enemy fire by wrapping it up in mattresses and bales of wool.

Santa Maria del Carmine

The church, begun in 1268, houses some of Florence's most important frescoes in the Brancacci Chapel. They were commissioned from Masolino and his pupil Masaccio by a wealthy merchant in 1423. Masaccio died in Rome, aged 27, before his work was completed, and the finial scenes were painted by Filippino Lippi. Masaccio's luminous colours, his expressive figures, his use of light and space all herald the Renaissance (see in particular *The Expulsion of Adam and Eve from the Garden of Eden.*) Many other artists found inspiration in these frescoes, including Michelangelo who came as a student to sketch the figures.

Santo Spirito

Brunelleschi designed this church for the Augustinian order, while the belfry is the work of Baccio d'Agnolo (1503). Inside you can see paintings by Filippino Lippi. In the refectory of the original monastery (entrance at no. 29) are two fine 14th-century frescoes of the *Last Supper* and the *Crucifixion*, by Orcagna or one of his pupils.

The church looks onto the shady little Piazzo Santo Spirito, very lively in the mornings (except Sunday) when housewives buy their fruit and vegetables at the market stalls.

Fiesole

Quite apart from its own charms, one of the principal attractions of this classical Tuscan hill town is the romantic view it commands over green, often misty wooded slopes of the Arno valley to the city of Florence 8 km (5 miles) to the southwest. Etruscan citadel, *Faesulae* to the Romans, Fiesole was much appreciated by the Medici as a place to escape to from the Florentine summer cauldron. Its heyday came in the 18th and 19th centuries as aristocratic villas mushroomed among splendid hillside gardens.

Just south of town is the 15th-century monastery church of San Domenico, with a porticoed façade added in 1635. An early triptych of Fra Angelico stands in the first chapel to the left.

On the town's main square, Piazza Mino de Fiesole, the most distinctive element of the much renovated Romanesque cathedral is its crenellated 13th-century campanile. Uphill, behind the bishop's palace (Palazzo Vescovile) the church of San Francesco stands on the site of the ancient Etruscan acropolis, with nearby public gardens offering the most majestic of Fiesole's many views.

North of the cathedral you can see fragments of the Etruscan city's walls, a Roman temple built on Etruscan foundations and a Roman amphitheatre.

23

For many people, it is the vineyards and sunny hilltop villages of the Chianti region that represent the very essence of Tuscany. After a drive through the wine country, you can follow up wine-tastings with the cultural attractions of San Casciano, Boccaccio's hometown of Certaldo and the monuments of Volterra and San Gimignano.

Via Chiantigiana

The wine route, along highway 222 south from Florence, is sign-posted by the jolly *Gallo Nero* (Black Cockerel) of the region's most prestigious Chianti Classico labels. It leads through a totally enchanting landscape to some of the more heart-warming achievements of Italian civilization. The September and October harvest *(vendemmia)* is the occasion for lively wine festivals, but tasting and buying in the major centres is possible throughout the year.

Impruneta

This farming village just outside Florence marks the northern end of the wine route. Its produce includes delicious table grapes, celebrated in a late September festival which is followed by the mid-October *fiera di San Luca*, a major agricultural fair for cattle, horses and dairy products. Over the centuries, Impruneta's farm-land has provided the fine clay used by the Renaissance terracotta workshops of the Della Robbia family and now for modern pottery, figurines and decorative tiles. In the centre of town on Piazza Buondelmonti, you will see Luca Della Robbia's glazed terracotta figures in the Basilica of Santa Maria all'Impruneta. A Crucifixion and saints Peter and Paul decorate two 15th-century chapels behind the main altar. The church itself has retained its fortified Romanesque campanile behind the now largely baroque nave and portico.

Greve

The route down to this major wine-distribution centre and market town follows the meandering Greve river, passing on the way the first Chianti vineyards and several medieval castles. The Castello di Verrazzano belonged to the family of the 16th-century navigator whose name now

San Gimignano's Piazza della Cisterna is named for its travertine well.

HIGHLIGHTS

- **Via Chiantigiana**: for the joy of its landscapes and taste of its wines
- **San Gimignano**: magical skyline of medieval towers
- **Volterra**: proud Palazzo dei Priori in ancient Etruscan town

graces a bridge at the entrance to New York harbour—which he explored in 1524. Giovanni's family name reappears—with his statue—on Greve's attractively arcaded main piazza.

The wine shops here give you a good opportunity to compare labels and prices of the region's best vintages.

East of town, the fortified hilltop village of Montefioralle was the feudal stronghold of the Vespucci family, whose descendant Amerigo left his name on a whole continent. The church of Santo Stefano has a 12th-century triptych by Bicci di Lorenzo.

Panzano

The hilltop terrace of this modest but charming village commands a superb view of the broad *Conca d'Oro* (golden shell) embraced by an undulating ridge. Guarded by tall dark cypresses, the green vineyards and silver olive groves 26 are dotted with honey- or russet-coloured villas and farmhouses— a painter's delight. An imposing gateway and two wings of the castle survive from Panzano's fortifications destroyed in 15th-century battles between Medici and papal armies.

Castellina

On a densely wooded hill 578 m (1.896 ft) above sea level, this ancient Etruscan citadel is dominated by formidable medieval fortifications with a splendid view of three valleys—Elsa to the west, Pesa to the north and Arbia to the east. Many of the 15th- and 16th-century houses have been well restored, notably the Renaissance Palazzo Ugolini with its rusticated ashlar-stone façade. The town hall is housed in the 14th-century Rocca castle-keep.

North of town on Montecalvario, looking out over the Val d'Elsa, are four Etruscan tombs dating back to the 6th century BC. (Their sculpture, jewellery, ceramics are now displayed in the archaeological museums of Florence and Chiusi.)

Radda

After Castellina, the wine route leaves highway 222 and continues east along 429 to a 14th-century Florentine stronghold in the middle of Siena's communal territory. Radda has kept its medieval layout in an elongated ellipse.

On the façade of the 15th-century communal Palazzo del Podestà are coats of arms of the town's feudal lords and a fresco of the Madonna and Child. The Franciscan convent of Santa Maria al Prato is being transformed into a museum of paintings and sculpture from the region's churches, notably a 14th-century polyptych by Benardo Daddi. The town's Chianti historical research centre *(Centro di Studi storici chiantigiani)* has a small wine museum.

La Badia di Coltibuono

Set in an oak and pine forest 6 km (4 miles) east of Radda, the 11th-century Benedictine monastery was left in ruin by papal armies and has now been restored and converted into wine cellars and a gourmet restaurant.

Gaiole

This major wine-tasting centre rises from a lovely green landscape of wooded hills and vineyards. Immediately west of the town's historic centre are two sets of medieval buildings: the simple 13th-century Romanesque parish church of Santa Maria a Spaltenna, with an adjacent castle tower now converted into a hotel; and, at least 200 years older, the imposing fortress of Vertine. Also in the vicinity are a flour mill and spinning mill once operated by the abbots of Coltibuono.

Castello di Meleto

South of Gaiole, this massive but elegant Renaissance castle stands at the centre of a highly esteemed Chianti Classico vineyard. The owners are justly proud of the castle's delightful little 18th-century theatre and may be persuaded to show it to visitors.

Castello di Brolio

Like nearby Meleto, this castle is the property of the Ricasoli family, whose vineyards and olive groves have been here over 900 years. Standing at the end of a handsome avenue of cypresses, the 19th-century neo-Gothic pile, more palazzo than fortress, is a reconstruction of what was originally a Renaissance edifice by Florentine architect Giuliano da Sangallo. From the 15th-century fortifications there is a magnificent view over the Arbia valley to Siena and the hills of Volterra.

San Casciano

Overlooking the southern approaches to Florence, the hill town of San Casciano in Val di Pesa had its medieval defenses reinforced by the Medici in the 15th century—still visible today. Two museums have important works of art: in the Misericordia, a *Crucifixion* (1325) by Simone Martini and a pulpit (1339) sculpted by Giovanni di Balduccio; and in the Arte Sacra, *Arch-* 27 *angel Michael* by Coppa di Marcovaldo and a *Madonna and Child* by Ambrogio Lorenzetti.

Certaldo

A 19th-century statue of Giovanni Boccaccio, the celebrated 14th-century author of *The Decameron*, stands in the square bearing his name in the lower town, Certaldo Basso. His home was in the more attractive upper town, the fortified medieval Certaldo Alto, at Via Boccaccio 18. The family house with tower and loggia is now a museum and Boccaccio research centre.

At the top of the town, above the fine Renaissance Palazzo Pretorio, the garden terrace has a good view over the Val d'Elsa to the towers of San Gimignano.

San Gimignano

From whichever point you approach this town, you can understand its time-honoured name of San Gimignano dalle Belle Torri. Those rectangular "Beautiful Towers" stand out on the horizon, pink in the morning, golden in the afternoon, like an army of dignified stone sentinels. In the Middle Ages there were over 70 of them, built ever higher in a status contest between rival families guarding Florence's southern frontiers with the commune of Siena. After Florentine supremacy no longer depended on this strategic outpost, most of the towers were dismantled or just collapsed. A dozen of them, mostly nearly 800 years old, dominate the *centro storico*.

Via San Giovanni

Beyond Porta San Giovanni, the town's handsome southern gateway, this street of medieval patrician houses and hostelries offers a first glimpse of the city centre's landmark towers. The houses on Via San Giovanni have been converted into shops and galleries, the old Romanesque church of San Francesco now a wine shop featuring San Gimignano's own white Vernaccia.

Piazza della Cisterna

Brick-paved in a herringbone pattern, this is the first of two adjoining squares forming the city's *centro storico* bordered by its 13th-century towers. A travertine stone well *(Cisterna)* gives the piazza its name. Opposite, to the left of the Arco dei Becci leading into the piazza, are the twin Ardinghelli towers.

Piazza del Duomo

Soaring over the cathedral is the town's tallest surviving tower, the Torre Grossa, 54 m (177 ft), part of the striking Palazzo del Populo (1288). Once a seat of communal government, it now houses in its Museo Civico a *Crucifixion* by

WINE IN CHIANTI

Among the many achievements of the great Medici dynasty, certainly not least important was the protection of the Chianti wine label. Cosimo III, Grand Duke of Tuscany, passed in 1716 what was probably the first law to register a wine region's trademark. The vineyards authorized to use the label covered roughly the same 70,000 hectares as the modern Chianti region.

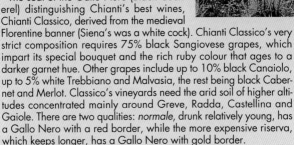

Tuscany had produced wine since Etruscan times, but Chianti vineyards were always held in high esteem, becoming the much prized spoils of medieval battles between Florence and Siena. In 1415 Florence asserted its ascendancy by founding the Chianti League (Lega del Chianti) with Radda as its capital. The Ricasoli family's Brolio vineyard became a battlefield in wars between papal and Medici forces, which left its castello in ruins in 1478. Four centuries later, Bettino Ricasoli modernized his vineyards and, as one of newly united Italy's first prime ministers, developed national commerce and transportation to the great benefit of Chianti's wine production.

The seal of the Gallo Nero (Black Cockerel) distinguishing Chianti's best wines, Chianti Classico, derived from the medieval Florentine banner (Siena's was a white cock). Chianti Classico's very strict composition requires 75% black Sangiovese grapes, which impart its special bouquet and the rich ruby colour that ages to a darker garnet hue. Other grapes include up to 10% black Canaiolo, up to 5% white Trebbiano and Malvasia, the rest being black Cabernet and Merlot. Classico's vineyards need the arid soil of higher altitudes concentrated mainly around Greve, Radda, Castellina and Gaiole. There are two qualities: *normale*, drunk relatively young, has a Gallo Nero with a red border, while the more expensive *riserva*, which keeps longer, has a Gallo Nero with gold border.

Only three quarters of the Classico vineyards are registered with the European Union. The others produce the quite honorable "table red" Chianti, sometimes with the faint hint of a sparkle.

The hill town of Volterra is a treasure trove of Etruscan, Roman and medieval art and architecture.

Coppa di Marcovaldo (1260), two paintings of the *Annunciation* (1482) by Filippino Lippi, as well as major works by Benozzo Gozzoli and Pinturicchio. Across the square, with a tower just slightly shorter, is the earlier seat of government, Palazzo del Podestà (1239), which recently restored its 18th-century theatre.

Collegiata

The collegiate church is also known as "duomo" though without cathedral status. This bare-façaded 12th-century Romanesque edifice has a rich collection of art treasures in its interior. On the west wall, sculptures of *Arch-*angel Gabriel and *Mary Annunciate* (1421) by Siena's Jacopo della Quercia, and *Last Judgment* frescoes (1393) by Taddeo di Bartolo; 14th-century frescoes of the *Old Testament* in the north aisle and the *New Testament* in the south; and a splendid Renaissance chapel with elegant frescoes (1475) by Florentine Domenico Ghirlandaio.

Rocca di Montestàffoli

For a grand view over southern Tuscany, make your way behind the Collegiata up to the ruins of Florentine fortifications erected in 1358, set now in a public park. The top of the tower offers a magical panorama of terraced vineyards, majestic cypresses and olive groves.

Volterra

Some 50 km (30 miles) south-west of San Gimignano, this proud old Etruscan city, the last to fall to the Romans in 90 BC, shares the rugged charm of its surrounding hill country. Etruscan foundations support the medieval city walls, and sculpted heads of three Etruscan deities are inserted in the ancient town's western gate, Porta all'Arco. Two archaeological sites bear witness to the Etruscan-Roman era.

On the southeast side of town, near the Renaissance Fortezza, now a maximum security prison, is an acropolis with temple remains and huge cisterns dating back to the 3rd century BC. On the north side is a Roman theatre with Corinthian columns (1st century AD).

Piazza dei Priori

This superb medieval square expresses Volterra's civic dignity with the lofty fortress-like Palazzo dei Priori (1208), Tuscany's oldest surviving town hall. Its laws were enforced by police who were headquartered across the piazza in the triple-arched Palazzo Pretorio, whose daunting Torre del Podestà served as a dungeon.

Duomo

The Pisan-style design of the sober Romanesque cathedral is believed to have been completed in the 13th century by Nicola Pisano. Among its major works of art is a fine polychrome wood *Deposition* (1228), also probably Pisan, in a chapel off the south transept. Two 15th-century sculptures of angels on columns either side of the main altar are works of Mino da Fiesole. In front of the Duomo is an octagonal 13th-century baptistery, partly clad in green and white marble. In the bare interior to the right of the altar is a font fashioned from an Etruscan memorial stone with bas-reliefs carved in 1502 by Andrea Sansovino.

Museo Etrusco Guarnacci

Occupying the Palazzo Desideri-Tangassi on Via Don Minzoni 15, this museum is one of Italy's most important collections of Etruscan art. Its works, many dating back to the 7th century BC, include bronze and stone sculpture, funeral urns in alabaster and terracotta, jewellery and ceramics.

Pinacoteca

The art museum, Via dei Sarti 1, boasts a splendid *Deposition* (1521) by Mannerist master Rosso Fiorentino, along with works by Taddeo di Bartolo, Luca Signorelli and Ghirlandaio.

31

➤ SIENA AND SURROUNDINGS

Siena, Monteriggioni, Crete senesi, Montalcino,
Sant'Antimo, San Quirico d'Orcia, Pienza, Montepulciano

Siena and its environs have all the rich warm colour of the "burnt sienna" to be found in any self-respecting paint-box, the colour of the south Tuscan earth used in terracotta pottery and sculpture. They reflect something of the passions of Siena's celebrated hotly contested Palio horse race. Many find Siena more sensual, even feminine, than the somewhat dispassionate, rather masculine Florence. Similarly, contrasting with Florence's greener hinterland, the Sienese hill country, particularly to the south, lends an almost scorched quality to its dramatic, otherworldly landscapes.

Siena

History and geography have combined to give Siena its unique charm. Because it submitted to the Florence-led duchy in 1559, the city's superb Gothic and Renaissance monuments were spared destruction in Tuscany's power struggles. Siena sits astride a ridge that forks across not one but three hilltops, giving the *centro storico* a fascinating array of winding streets and sloping piazzas, again in stark contrast to Florence's formal right-angled grid plan laid out in the plain in Roman times.

Piazza del Campo

At the point where the city's three hills meet on the Y-shaped ridge, the curved and sloping piazza takes the form of a scallop shell. This was where the Romans built their forum. For centuries it has been the centre of political meetings and riots, festivities and public hangings, and it is still the stage of the world-famous Palio, the major event in Tuscany's tourist calendar. In the shadow of the Palazzo Pubblico, seat of communal government, the piazza's herringbone-patterned redbrick paving was divided in the 14th century by white stone lines into nine segments, each allotted to the supporters of the nine city elders.

A white marble fountain, Fonte Gaia (1409), by sculptor Jacopo della Quercia, stands at the rear of the Campo. The carved reliefs of biblical scenes and Christian allegories are 19th-century replicas of the originals, now in the Palazzo Pubblico museum.

*Siena's cathedral,
a gleaming marble gem
in a terracotta setting.*

33

Palazzo Pubblico

Like most Tuscan Gothic city halls, this one's tower and battlements make it look at first like a fortress, but the curve of its russet-hued façade (1310) embraces the Campo's contours to add a typically more "feminine" Sienese touch. And the delicate triple-mullioned windows of the council chambers and the elegant arcade below could never have withstood a serious enemy assault.

HIGHLIGHTS

- **Siena**: the Palazzo Pubblico on Piazza del Campo, the Duomo and Pinacoteca art museum
- **Monteriggioni**: wonderfully preserved fortifications
- **Crete senesi**: a lunar landscape south of Siena
- **Montalcino**: charming hill town, home of Brunello wine
- **Sant'Antimo**: Romanesque Benedictine abbey-church
- **Pienza**: Pope Pius II's elegant Renaissance home town
- **Montepulciano**: more fine wines in cellars of Renaissance palazzi, with magnificent San Biagio church down the hill

The same grace characterizes the Torre della Mangia, a lofty symbol of civic pride rising 102 m (334 ft) over the Campo. Its first bell-ringer left the tower an abbreviated version of his nickname, Mangiaguadagni (Money-glutton). From the observation deck, 503 steps up, share his wonderful view of the Tuscan vineyards and hills. The chapel at the foot of the tower commemorated deliverance from the Black Death of 1348. Its arcade is a Renaissance addition.

Museo Civico

The richly endowed municipal museum is housed in the upper council chambers of the Palazzo Pubblico. The museum's main masterpieces are located in three of the chambers.

In the Sala del Mappamondo (named after Ambrogio Lorenzetti's now completely faded map of Siena's international banking interests) is Simone Martini's exquisite *Maestà* (1315) fresco of the enthroned Madonna. Opposite, also attributed to Simone Martini, is a ceremonial fresco of condottiere *Guidoriccio da Fogliano* leading Sienese forces to victory.

The Sala della Pace (Hall of Peace), the chamber of the town's Nine Patricians, has beautifully detailed frescoes (1339) by Ambrogio Lorenzetti, one a grim allegory of *Bad Government* and two devoted to *Good Government*—Siena's, of course.

The Sala del Concistorio has a fine marble portal (1448) by Bernard Rossellino. Domenico Beccafumi's Mannerist allegorical ceiling frescoes (1535) extol such ancient republican virtues as Patriotism, Justice and Concord.

Up in the second-floor Loggia are Jacopo della Quercia's original 15th-century carvings, barely recognizable, for the Piazza del Campo's fountain, along with a great view over the city.

Via di Città

Curving west from the Croce del Travaglio at the rear of the Piazza del Campo, this was Siena's Wall Street, where some of the world's leading bankers and financiers built their splendid palazzi in the 14th and 15th centuries.

At the beginning of the street is the Loggia della Mercanzia, a Renaissance arcade that served as a commercial tribunal to arbitrate disputes from all over Europe.

Via di Città 89 is the battlemented redbrick Gothic-Renaissance Palazzo Chigi-Saracini. It was the home of a banking dynasty who, in their 15th-century heyday, were much more powerful than the Medici, as they dispensed credit and counsel to kings and popes, and subsequently providing two Chigi popes, Julius III and Alexander VII. In 1932, Count Guido Chigi-Saracini created an internationally renowned music academy in the palazzo, which now stages summer concerts and exhibitions of the family art collection, highlighted by Sassetta's *Epiphany* and *St Martin*.

At Via di Città 126, the façade of the Palazzo Piccolomini (1495) is more Florentine than Sienese in its austere Renaissance restraint, relieved by some decorative upper windows. It was the home of Caterina Piccolomini, sister of Pope Pius II, and as seat of the Bank of Italy continues to observe the street's tradition.

Duomo

Theatrically raised on a stage-like platform, the grandiose Gothic cathedral, just like the Palazzo Pubblico, asserts Siena's high opinion of itself in the Middle Ages. The municipality stamped its heraldic colours on the black and white marble bands of the walls. Standing on the site of an ancient Roman temple to Minerva, the Duomo reaffirms a historic bond between Siena and Rome with emblematic sculptures on two columns flanking its façade. Like Rome's Romulus and Remus, so Siena's legendary founders Senius and Aschius are shown as twin boys being suckled by a she-wolf. The originals 35

ON AND OFF TRACK AT THE PALIO

Since 1147, the Sienese have always staged their horse race, Corsa del Palio as a summer enactment of the year-round neighbourhood (*contrada*) rivalries. Each *contrada*—there are 17 in all, but only 10 compete each year, chosen on a rotation system—has its own meet-

ing-hall, oratory chapel and museum, and its own emblem appearing on a colourful banner: Eagle, Caterpillar, Snail, Owl, Dragon, Giraffe, Porcupine, Unicorn, She-Wolf, Scallop Shell, Goose, Ocean Wave, Panther, Forest, Tortoise, Tower, Mountain Goat. Race days (July 2 and August

16) come after several weeks of parties, training runs, street games, noisy parades mocking rivals. Hatred is stoked by ancient insults and injuries. Then each *contrada* gathers for an eve-of-race banquet, with horse and jockey at the head of the table.

Historians believe the Palio originated in Etruscan pagan revelries, but the event is now resolutely Christian. In the stables, an illuminated effigy of each *contrada*'s patron saint hangs over the horse's feed-box. On the way to the Campo, horse and jockey stop off for the priest's blessing at the *contrada* chapel.

The Palio starts with a pageant around the Campo of Renaissance-costumed standard-bearers from all 17 neighbourhoods and the grand *Sbandierata* of twirling and tossing the colourful emblematic flags. At last, the ten horses and their jockeys in the livery of each *contrada*'s colours appear from the Palazzo Pubblico's inner courtyard.

The race itself is as vicious as the old neighbourhood rivalries. Jockeys ride bareback, whip their opponents as much as their own horses and may, to honour a pre-race bribe, just slow down to deliberately block a rival's mount and let another horse through. Although the Campo is strewn with sawdust and its walls cushioned with mattresses, the track is as brutally dangerous as an ancient Roman chariot race, with both horses and jockeys frequently maimed. The winner is the first horse past the post after three laps, with or without its jockey. Siena's inveterate gamblers will tell you it does not matter if the race is fixed; the fun comes from betting on what the fix is. The Palio really does reflect the spirit of medieval Siena.

of these, like Giovanni Pisano's sculptures of patriarchs, prophets and philosophers on the façade, are kept in the Cathedral Museum. The garish Venetian mosaics in the façade's upper gables were added in 1877. The campanile (1313), with six tiers of mullioned windows, rises majestically above the right transept, which has a Donatello *Madonna* sculpted relief over the doorway.

The even more striking interior continues the black and white marble motif on its clustered columns. The floor has inlaid marble paving of 56 biblical and allegorical pictures composed by over 40 artists from 1369 to 1547, notably Domenico Beccafumi, Pinturicchio and Matteo di Giovanni.

Leading off the left aisle, the 16th-century Piccolomini Library traces with Pinturicchio's frescoes (1495) the life of Enea Silvio Piccolomini, later Pope Pius II. The library was founded by his nephew Francesco who himself became Pope Pius III—for just ten days.

In the left transept, sculptor Nicola Pisano's octagonal pulpit (1268), a masterpiece of medieval art, was carved with the aid of his nephew Giovanni and Arnolfo di Cambio.

In the right transept, Bernini's Chigi Chapel is a truly baroque monument with disconcerting marble sculptures of a voluptuous Mary Magdalene and ecstatic St Jerome at the entrance.

Baptistery

Accessible by stairs from the right transept exit to the Duomo Nuovo, the unfinished 14th-century octagonal edifice was built below the cathedral apse. It boasts an impressive baptismal font (1434) designed by Jacopo della Quercia. Besides his marble sculpture of *John the Baptist*, bronze reliefs include Ghiberti's *Christ's Baptism* and Donatello's *Herod's Banquet*.

Museo dell'Opera del Duomo

The Cathedral Museum is housed in the Duomo Nuovo, the shell of a 14th-century structure extending beyond the cathedral's right transept. This was part of an overambitious programme to compete with the cathedral being built by Florence, abandoned after the Black Death of 1348 and general decline in Siena's fortunes.

On the ground floor are Giovanni Pisano's 12 sculptures from the Duomo façade, in particular Miriam, sister of Moses, and basreliefs by Donatello and Jacopo della Quercia. Two masterpieces to see on the first floor are Duccio di Buoninsegna's *Madonna Enthroned* (*Maestà*, 1311) and Pietro Lorenzetti's *Birth of the Madonna* (1342).

Santa Maria della Scala Hospital

Opposite the cathedral stairs, the monumental medieval hospital founded for the poor and abandoned children has been transformed into a cultural centre. In the vast Sala del Pellegrinaio (Pilgrimage Hall), detailed frescoes, mainly by Domenico di Bartolo, provide a fascinating insight into hospital methods and costumes in the 15th century. The hospital church has several fine sculptures, including a bronze *Christ Resurrected* (1476) by Lorenzo Vecchietta on the main altar.

Among other recent cultural installations, the city's Archaeological Museum assembles private regional collections to display sculpture, ceramics, coins and jewellery dating back to the Villanovan culture (9th century BC), Etruscan and ancient Roman tombs.

Pinacoteca Nazionale

South of Via di Città, Siena's great gallery of painting is housed in the noble 15th-century late-Gothic Palazzo Buonsignori (Via San Pietro 29) and the adjacent slightly older Palazzo Brigido. Five centuries of the city's art offer a charming study in the rich colour, soft light and gentle atmosphere that marked the work of Sienese painters. They include Guido da Siena, Duccio di Buoninsegna, *Madonna of the Franciscans* (1290); Simone Martini, *Agostino Novello* (1324); Pietro Lorenzetti, *Crucifixion* (1326); his brother Ambrogio, *Annunciation* (1344); Giovanni di Paolo, *Last Judgment* (1460); Sassetta, *Last Supper* (1424); Domenico Beccafumi, *St Catherine Receiving Stigmata* (1515); Sodoma, *Jesus on the Column* (1511). Among the few non-Sienese artists: Albrecht Dürer, *St Jerome*; Paris Bordone, *Annunciation*; Lorenzo Lotto, *Nativity*; Quentin Metsys, *Elizabeth of England*.

Sant'Agostino

South from the Pinacoteca Nazionale along Via San Pietro, the church is worth a visit even when closed for the superb terrace view over the city and its gardens. Inside, its art treasures include a Perugino *Crucifixion*, Sodoma's *Epiphany* over the main altar and an Ambrogio Lorenzetti fresco in the Piccolomini Chapel.

Santa Maria dei Servi

Tucked away in an almost rustic setting on the southeast corner of town just beyond the old Jewish Ghetto, this is a simple, unadorned Romanesque-Gothic church with some impressive art works: Coppo di Marcovaldo's *Madonna del Bordone* (1261), and Niccolò di Segna's *Massacre of the Innocents* (1491).

San Domenico
Northwest of the city centre is the Camollìa neighbourhood where Caterina Benincasa, later St Catherine, grew up. San Domenico is the 14th-century Gothic fortress-church in which she prayed and frequently experienced visions of Mary, Jesus and the saints. Caterina was an ardent nurse to Siena's plague-victims and underdogs. Her best-known charge was Niccolò Tuldo, whom she comforted with prayer in his last days before execution for a small but capital crime. In ecstasy at the scaffold, she caught his severed head in her lap, and told her mother in a letter: "I derived such joy from the perfume of this blood that I would not let anyone remove what had spattered on my clothes."

In the Vaulted Chapel at the church's west end is Andrea Vanni's portrait of her (1414), said to be the one true physical likeness, showing her in a characteristic state of ecstasy. Off the right aisle, St Catherine's Chapel is decorated with Sodoma's celebrated frescoes of her. The saint's head is kept in a Renaissance reliquary at the altar.

Monteriggioni
Surrounded by olive groves and vineyards just 15 km (9 miles) north of Siena, this enchanting little hill town has preserved its almost circular 13th-century fortifications. The 14 lookout bastions, compared to giants in Dante's *Divine Comedy*, were built as part of Siena's early-warning system against Florentine attack.

Crete senesi
The country southeast of Siena is marked by "crests" *(crete)* of clay eroded over the ages into a dramatic desert of parched hillocks and ravines, broken only by an occasional stand of dark green cypresses. It is a landscape that inspired painters like Duccio, Lorenzetti and Giovanni di Paolo, and perhaps also poet Dante for his *Inferno*.

Asciano
This hill town 26 km (16 miles) southeast of Siena is a medieval oasis in the *Crete* desert. Within its ramparts, rebuilt in the 15th century, is the simple Romanesque Basilica di Sant'Agata with blind-arcaded façade, crenellated campanile and octagonal dome. In the oratory chapel left of the basilica, the Museum of Sacred Art has important works executed by 14th- and 15th-century Sienese artists for local churches, including paintings by Matteo di Giovanni and the Maestro dell' Osservanza and a polychrome *Annunciation* sculpture by Francesco di Valdambrino. On Via Matteotti, the Etruscan Museum

displays an interesting collection of jewellery, terracotta figurines, ceramics and bronzes from the Poggio Pinci necropolis (7th century BC).

Monte Oliveto Maggiore

The 14th-century Benedictine monastery stands on a rocky ridge 9 km (5 miles) south of Asciano, in a beautiful park of cypresses, pines, oaks and olive trees. In the Great Cloister are frescoes (1498–1508) by Sodoma and Luca Signorelli tracing the life of St Benedict, and there are two other pictures by Sodoma at the entrance to the abbey-church: *Jesus Carrying the Cross* (left) and *Jesus on the Column* (right). The nave's choir stalls (1505), decorated by Giovanni da Verona with birds, fountains and views of Siena, count among Italy's most admirable works of inlaid wood carving.

Montalcino

In the rolling country south of the *Crete*, this enchanting fortified hill town gives you a chance to taste its famous Brunello red wine on the spot.

Dominated by the soaring clock tower of its Palazzo dei Priori, the medieval Piazza del Popolo has a decidedly Sienese air to it, except for a statue of Florence's Duke Cosimo I de' Medici in the palazzo portico. The duke added the formidable ramparts to the town's 14th-century Rocca fortress, ideal for a view over the southern Tuscan hills. A wine-cellar *(Enoteca)* in the castle keep offers the local wines for tasting and purchase.

At Via Ricasoli 29, the Museo Civico groups art and archaeological collections. Highlights include Madonnas attributed to Pietro Lorenzetti and Simone Martini and a finely sculpted polychrome *St Peter Enthroned* by Francesco di Valdambrino.

Sant'Antimo

The 12th-century Benedictine abbey-church built of honey-coloured travertine, 10 km (6 miles) south of Montalcino, enjoys an exquisite setting amid olive groves and stands of holm oak. Quite unlike other Tuscan churches, this masterpiece of Romanesque architecture was designed in the French Cistercian tradition with its cluster of domed chapels for the apse, built over a 9th-century crypt. (The monastery claims to have been founded by Charlemagne in 781.) The four-square campanile is in Lombard style, but the exterior's sculpted animals and birds, like the capitals with biblical scenes or floral and geometric patterns on the interior's columns, are believed to be the work of French sculptors. Semi-translucent onyx and alabaster in the bases of the columns gives the nave a delicate luminosity. Over the main altar, notice also the fine 12th-century wooden *Crucifixion*, probably Burgundian.

San Quirico d'Orcia

This hospitable fortified town 15 km (9 miles) east of Montalcino was a major stop for north European pilgrims journeying to Rome in the Middle Ages. Welcoming travellers on the Siena road at the entrance to town is its handsome Romanesque Collegiate church. The two gabled portals portray the dangers and sinful temptations of life's journey with

sculptures of killer crocodiles and alluring sirens. Inside, notice the Sano di Pietro triptych in the left transept. Antonio Barili's fine inlaid wood choir stalls (1502) were brought here from Siena's Duomo.

On Piazza della Libertà, enjoy the view of the Orcia valley from the 16th-century Leonini Gardens, laid out by Diomede Leone in the geometric Italian Renaissance style.

Pienza

Once the quiet country village of Corsignano, 10 km (6 miles) east of San Quirico, the birthplace of Enea

Sant'Antimo is particularly known for Gregorian chant, which resounds beautifully from its "singing stone".

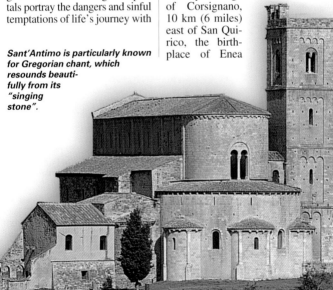

Silvio Piccolomini was transformed after he became Pope Pius II into an "ideal city", a unique experiment in Renaissance urban planning that took just three years (1459–62).

As redesigned by Bernardo Rossellino, Pienza has all the tenets of classical proportion and formal harmony laid down by his master, Leon Battista Alberti. The Florentine architect uses sloping pavement, oblique angles and cleverly nuanced proportions in the surrounding palazzi and cathedral to make the central Piazza Pio II look more spacious than it really is.

Cattedrale

The church's only ornament on its classical Renaissance façade is the pope's garlanded coat of arms high above the main entrance. An octagonal campanile, more Gothic in inspiration, rises discreetly at the rear. The interior gains space and light by audaciously (and precariously) extending the choir out over the Orcia valley, with a great rear window bringing unobstructed light into the nave.

In a chapel left of the choir is Lorenzo Vecchietta's *Assumption of Mary* (1461).

Museo Diocesano

The museum of the cathedral's art treasures was recently moved to the bishop's palace (Palazzo Vescovile) on the left side of the piazza as you stand facing the cathedral. Built as the residence of Cardinal Rodrigo Borgia (later Pope Alexander VI), the palace now houses major paintings by Pietro Lorenzetti, Bartolo di Fredi and Fra Bartolomeo, together with three superb Flemish tapestries and the renowned 14th-century ceremonial cope of Pope Pius II, lavishly crafted by English weavers.

Palazzo Piccolomini

Fronted by Rossellino's beautifully carved travertine well, the residence of Pius II has an elegant dignity; the façade's only ornament being mullioned windows. Its square Corinthian-columned courtyard leads on the left to a Hanging Garden laid out above a three-tiered loggia. This exemplary piece of Italian Renaissance landscaping has a magnificent view over the Orcia valley.

Pieve di Corsignano

Take a delightful 10-minute walk past farmhouses west of town to the humble Romanesque parish church where the future pope was baptised in 1405. A twin-tailed siren was carved over the main entrance of the 11th-century round-towered church, to warn the little Piccolomini of future temptations. His baptismal font is still inside.

Montepulciano

Connoisseurs place this hill town's Vino Nobile among the best wines in Tuscany, up there with the Chianti Classico Brolio and Brunello di Montalcino. It can be tasted in the wine-cellars of the town's splendid Renaissance palaces, built after Florence asserted its supremacy in the 15th and 16th centuries. The Medici had Antonio da Sangallo the Elder erect new fortifications, including the monumental Porta al Prato gateway at the north end of town.

Via di Gracciano del Corso

The town's finest Renaissance palazzi line the main street leading up to the city centre, notably Palazzo Avignonesi (No. 91) and Palazzo Bucelli (No. 73), the latter with Etruscan urns built into its façade. Michelozzo added a Renaissance marble façade to the originally Gothic church of Sant'Agostino. The street enters the market square, Piazza delle Erbe, site of the grain merchants' 16th-century Loggia.

Piazza Grande

The town's main square is dominated by its 14th-century Palazzo Comunale, a typical Tuscan city hall with a façade probably remodelled by Michelozzo in 1440. In front of Antonio da Sangallo's Palazzo Nobili-Tarugi stands a

---

PUSHING THE BARREL

Montepulciano's *Bravio delle Botti* is a sweatier version of Siena's Palio. On the last Sunday in August, the town's strongmen push 80-kg barrels *(botti)* up the steep and winding slope of Via di Gracciano del Corso. The competition celebrates the forthcoming wine harvest for the Vino Nobile. The loser gets to drink just as much as the winner.

Renaissance well, on which the emblematic griffins of Montepulciano are symbolically united with Florence's lions.

The Duomo has an unfinished and unprepossessing façade, but is worth a look inside for its baptistery with its finely carved font left of the entrance, and the Taddeo di Bartolo *Assumption* triptych (1401) over the main altar.

Church of San Biagio

Just southwest of town, Antonio da Sangallo erected what many consider to be the finest of all his Renaissance buildings. The church stands majestically on a platform at the end of an avenue of cypresses, the dome crowning the four equal arms of its Greek-cross ground plan. It was inaugurated in 1529 by Pope Clement VII, a Medici.

43

▶ AROUND PISA

Pisa, Livorno, Viareggio, Forte dei Marmi,
Marble Towns, Lucca, Montecatini Terme,
Collodi, Pistoia, Prato, Vinci, Empoli

That Leaning Tower is not just one of the world's greatest tourist magnets, it is also stunningly beautiful. It is in perfect harmony with the surrounding architecture of Pisa's great monuments and this architecture in turn influenced building throughout the region, even in the city's proud rivals of Lucca, Pistoia and Prato. Northern Tuscany's hills turn to mountains as they approach the Alps, most dramatically around the craggy quarries of Carrara that provided the marble for the monumental façades and many masterpieces of Italian art. Along the coast, Viareggio is the flagship of the Riviera.

Pisa

The matchless art treasures on what the city modestly calls its *Campo dei Miracoli* (Field of Miracles) are the tangible benefits of its vast medieval maritime empire. Cathedral, baptistery and campanile, better known as the Leaning Tower, were financed from profits brought back by legitimate merchants and ruthless buccaneers—often on the same ships. If you start early, you can visit the major monuments and museums in one day, at most two.

Piazza del Duomo

This blessed square on the north side of the city centre encompasses all the major stages in the life of pious Pisans. At birth, they receive their name in the baptistery. They take communion and get married in the cathedral. The bells of the campanile ring out the good news, and toll for their funeral. And they are buried in the Camposanto cemetery.

Duomo

The delicate ornament characterizing the Romanesque cathedral evokes the Pisan republic's commercial and cultural contacts with the eastern Mediterranean. The church incorporates Byzantine and Arabic design elements in the white marble façade's four-tiered arcades above the three porches. Andrea Pisano's Madonna tops the façade, flanked by two angels from the workshop of Giovanni Pisano. Building began in 1064, celebrating the defeat of the Arabs that secured Pisa's trading post in Sicily, and was complete

Pisa's Leaning Tower—an engineering disaster, but a triumph for tourism.

44

in 1118. Architect Buscheto's sarcophagus in the façade's far left arch bears the Latin inscription: "This marble church is without equal."

In the left aisle, Giovanni Pisano's masterful marble pulpit (1311) has sculpted reliefs of Old and New Testament scenes and the *Last Judgment*. On columns leading to the choir are Andrea del Sarto's 15th-century paintings of saints Catherine, Margaret, Peter and John the Baptist. In the apse vault, see the 13th-century mosaic of *Jesus the Redeemer* to which Cimabue added the head of the Apostle John.

Leaning Tower

Begun behind the cathedral in 1173, the campanile began listing in the sandy subsoil even before it was completed. Construction stopped for a century at the third storey and the tower was topped off with a belfry in 1301, still leaning. Since 1992, the tilt—about 5 m (16 ft) from true upright—has been halted. Architects, engineers and geologists have collaborated to strengthen foundations with a bolstering mixture of soil and cement and bind the tower-base and lower tiers with massive steel cables. But not to straighten it up—"Heaven forbid!" say the souvenir-sellers. Straight, the lovely six-tiered colonnaded campanile

would be 55 m (180 ft) high. After 11 years of work, the tower was finally re-opened to the public in late 2001.

Battistero

With its opulently curving dome, the circular baptistery makes a decidedly feminine counterpart to the angular cathedral. Begun as a largely Romanesque edifice in 1152 by architect Diotisalvi, who was also responsible for the Leaning Tower, the work was completed by Nicola and Giovanni Pisano, with Gothic decoration added to upper tiers, the crowning statue of John the Baptist and the biblical sculpture around the doorway.

The interior's grandiose marble pulpit (1260) is considered to be Nicola Pisano's personal masterpiece, with sculpture drawing on pagan models from Etruscan and Greco-Roman antiquity for his allegorical and biblical subjects. The octagonal baptismal font (1246) is a fine work of white marble and geometric mosaic inlay.

Camposanto

The original earth of the marble-cloistered cemetery is said to have been brought on Pisan ships from Jerusalem's Calvary, on the order of Archbishop Ubaldo Lanfranchi in 1203. The cemetery was built 75 years later in the form of an open-air three-aisle Gothic basilica. In a marble tabernacle in the wall facing the cathedral are biblical sculptures from the workshop of Giovanni Pisano.

American cannon fire in 1944 badly damaged the cemetery's 14th- and 15th-century frescoes, many still undergoing painstaking restoration, but some displayed along the north wall. At the west end of the cemetery, you can see sculpted Roman sarcophagi which were re-used here as coffins for Pisan Christians.

LEANING TOWARDS THE TRUTH

The delightful story that Pisa-born Galileo Galilei (1564–1642) went to the top of the Leaning Tower to test the velocity of falling weights is, sad to say, not true. He did, however, perform a valuable scientific experiment in the cathedral next door. Like many a teenager dragged into church to attend Mass, he found it difficult to pay attention. Instead, he gazed up at a heavy bronze lamp swinging from the ceiling and timed its oscillations against his pulse beats, arriving at the conclusion that a pendulum's timing remains constant however wide the swing. Back in church 50 years later, in Rome, he had to pay attention this time as the Inquisition's Holy Tribunal told him his proposition that the sun was the centre of the universe and that the earth moved around it "is absurd and false philosophically and formally heretical, because it is expressly contrary to the Holy Scripture". After leaving Pisa University, which he entered as a medical student in 1581, Galileo had indeed turned away from the Holy Scripture to develop the world's first astronomical telescope. He perfected this invention while working as professor of mathematics at the University of Padua (1592–1610). The telescope enabled him to confirm the truth of the Copernican solar system and to distinguish between stars (fixed) and planets (moving around the sun). At his last trial in 1633, the Church forced Galileo to abjure the evidence of his eyes and condemned him to lifelong house arrest in Florence. The observer of the universe continued his research, discovering, among others, the law that all bodies have weight. However, he went totally blind and died nine years later. The Vatican recognized the validity of his scientific work and rehabilitated him in 1992.

Museo dell'Opera del Duomo

The Cathedral Museum, housed in the Chapter House behind the Leaning Tower, assembles art works from the baptistery and Camposanto as well as the cathedral. Besides architectural fragments from these monuments, there are major sculptures by Giovanni Pisano and Sienese master Tino di Camaino, and a collection of Roman and Etruscan antiquities.

Museo di San Matteo

In a riverside Benedictine monastery, the museum exhibits Pisan sculpture from the 12th to 14th centuries, together with a bronze by Donatello and paintings by Gentile da Fabriano, Simone Martini, and a Masaccio *St Paul*, part of a polyptych for a Pisan Carmelite church.

Santa Maria della Spina

The thorn *(spina)* of the church's name is said to come from Jesus' crown and brought from Palestine by a Pisan merchant. To house it, a chapel on the Arno river's south bank was expanded into this charming white stone Gothic church looking for all the world like an ivory casket to house the relic. The side facing inland from the river has a series of porticoed tabernacles with statues of Jesus and his Apostles from Giovanni Pisano's workshop. (The thorn was moved to the Santa Chiara hospital chapel in the 19th century.)

Livorno

This now essentially modern city was scarcely more than an obscure little fishing village until the Dukes of Tuscany turned it into their major seaport in the 16th century. Today it is Italy's largest port for the container trade and fast growing for ferry and cruise passenger traffic.

Heavy World War II bombardments destroyed much of the *centro storico,* but a large part of the imposing fortifications have survived. Looming over the old harbour and indeed using it as a natural moat, the 16th-century

Sculpting marble at Pietrasanta near Carrara. Michelangelo used Pietra-santa stone for his Moses and Four Slaves.

Fortezza Vecchia (Old Fortress) was designed by Antonio da Sangallo, incorporating Duke Cosimo I's palace until it was destroyed in 1943.

Beside the Darsena Vecchia fishing harbour on Piazza Micheli is the town's most prominent monument, ostensibly to Ferdinando I but better known as the Monumento dei Quattro Mori (1607), for the bronzes of four Moorish slaves.

South along Viale Italia, the grand old Belle Epoque hotels recall the days when Livorno was an elegant seaside resort. It was also a pioneering 19th-century railway link to Pisa and Florence,

and its Stazione Centrale is a fine piece of Art Nouveau architecture—opposite a handsome old hotel on Piazza Dante.

Viareggio

With a sandy seashore long and straight as an arrow, the town has fulfilled its destiny as the classical Italian Riviera resort ever since Napoleon's beautiful sister built herself a holiday villa here in 1820. Eight years later, the town constructed its first wooden bathing huts and a seafront promenade. By the 1860s the resort had become internationally fashionable after British aristocrats arrived to promote the crazy new- 49 fangled idea of swimming in the sea and getting a suntan on the beach.

Just inland from the modern hotels and palm trees lining the seafront promenade is the more old-fashioned charm of Art Nouveau and Art Deco houses along Viale Michelangelo Buonarroti and Viale Foscolo. Here you will also find the lovely pinewoods of Pineta di Ponente (Western Pine Grove). Beyond the yachting harbour is the Pineta di Levante (Eastern Pine Grove).

South of town at Torre del Lago, Villa Puccini, where the composer of *Madame Butterfly* spent his last years, is a now a museum for his memorabilia.

Forte dei Marmi

Once a port to ship marble from the nearby Carrara quarries, the town is now the most elegant of Tuscany's Riviera resorts. More discreet than Viareggio, with romantic little hotels and smart villas tucked away behind luxuriant greenery, it appeals to well-off Florentine holiday-makers. Occasionally they emerge to head for relatively peaceful beaches and chic discos.

Marble Towns

In the foothills of the Apuan Alps east of the coast, the neighbouring towns of Massa and Carrara share the powers of provincial capital. From time immemorial, their economy has depended, at least in part, on their fabled marble quarries. Each has held onto enough of the marble to build some interesting monuments.

Massa

On the justly named Frigido river, the town, thoroughly modern today, was the fiefdom of the Malaspina dukes from the 15th to the 18th century. Their sprawling baroque Palazzo Cybo Malaspina (1705), now the seat of provincial government, dominates Piazza degli Aranci in the city centre. Orange and lemon trees were planted on the square in the 19th century.

Lavish use of the local marble can be seen in the cathedral's pretentious 20th-century white façade. Look in the baroque interior at the family's monumental tombs. In the Capella del Santo Sacramento in the right transept is a Pinturicchio fresco.

To the south, walk up to La Rocca, a medieval fortress to which the Malaspinas added a Renaissance palace and an 18th-century church. It has a great view over town and the Mediterranean.

Carrara

The town's name is forever linked to the world's finest white marble and the great artistic achievements of Roman Empire and Italian Renaissance. Sculptors still make it their home, many compete in the summer competition staged on the handsome marble-paved Piazza Alberica. In the shadow of 17th-century palazzi, they are given two weeks to create their own masterpiece.

The Pisan-style Romanesque and Gothic Duomo has a magnificent rose window in its marble façade. Housed in a 17th-century Malaspina palace, the Accademia di Belle Arte (Fine Arts Academy, Via Verdi) exhibits ancient Roman marble sculpture and reliefs. The Museo Civico del Marmo (Marble Museum, Viale XX Settembre) traces the history of marble quarrying and displays 300 different forms of marble from all over the world.

Carrara Quarries

Of the countless quarries in the valleys east of Carrara, the three most easy to visit are Fantiscritti, 6 km (4 miles) from town, with a little museum; Colonnata, 8 km (5 miles), for a good view close to the workers; and further north, Campo Cecina, 21 km (13 miles), for its superb mountain panoramas at an altitude of 1,350 m (4429 ft).

There are half a dozen different qualities and colours of marble: *Statuario*, the pure white that Michelangelo personally cut out for his *Pietà*; clear white *bianco chiaro*, considered good enough for household ornaments; light bluish-grey *bardiglio chiaro*; dark blue *bardiglio cupo*; yellowish *paonazza*; and green and white streaked *cipollino* ("spring onion").

WHICH WAY?

Little separates Massa and Carrara beyond their undying hostility. Nowhere in Tuscany is communal rivalry more fiercely alive. A Carrara tourist brochure explicitly protests: "Carrara is not Massa. Public and private offices and people continue to confuse one urban centre with the other, to the point where letters, telegrams and goods, even people, are directed to Massa instead of Carrara and vice versa." Carrara says Massa is envious because the marble is known worldwide only as Carrara marble. Massa replies that Carrara is jealous because Massa has successfully diversified its economy beyond the exploitation of marble. Whatever, arm yourself with good maps of the region. Local citizens are unlikely to tell you how to get from one place to the other.

Imaginative design on the façade of Lucca's San Michele in Foro—every column has a different pattern.

Lucca

Kept safe and sound for centuries within its ramparts, the *centro storico* makes this town one of the most attractive not only in Tuscany but in all of Italy. The fortunes its merchants made out of silk and banking are visible today in superb churches, palazzi and villas, which were carefully preserved from destruction with a slush fund set aside to bribe foreign invaders to bypass the town. The peaceful life nurtured many musicians—Luigi Boccherini and Giacomo Puccini were both born here. Today, the money still comes from textiles, but also shoes, paper-making, and agri-culture producing, among other things, the highest quality olive oil.

City Walls

For an overview of the old town and its monuments, start your tour with a walk along the top of the 16th-century fortifications. The complete promenade or *Passeggiata delle Mura* takes in 4 km (3 miles) around 11 tree-shaded bastions *(baluardi)* above grassy moats that offer a delightful setting for the town's summer music festival. In the northeast corner, Baluardo Cesare Battisti has a great view across to the Apuan Alps. To the southeast, Baluardo

San Regolo is now a children's playground and gateway to the Botanical Garden with a 200-year-old Chinese ginkgo and an American sequoia.

Duomo San Martino

The Romanesque cathedral seems to affirm the town's independent spirit by embedding its Lombard crenellated campanile in the Pisan-style porticoed façade, set beneath three tiers of polychrome marble arcades. Sculptures in the architrave of the north porch, *Annunciation, Adoration of the Magi* and *Deposition*, are attributed to Nicola Pisano.

Inside, to the right of the main entrance, is one of Tuscany's oldest Romanesque sculptures, a 12th-century equestrian statue of *St Martin and the Beggar*. Other art treasures include Jacopo della Quercia's sculpted sarcophagus for the tomb for Ilaria del Carretto (1408) in the left transept and on the main altar Ghirlandaio's *Madonna and Child with Saints*.

San Michele in Foro

Rising from the centre of the ancient Roman Forum, this exquisite Romanesque church, begun in 1070, elevated its tiered arcades to give a loftier impact to the typical Pisan façade. There is a wonderful variety to the colour and design of its columns—scrolled, chevroned, striped and sculpted, in green, pink, white or black marble. A 19th-century restoration added the sculpted heads of national heroes Garibaldi and Cavour to the third arcaded tier, on the third and fourth columns from the right (visible with binoculars).

Inside, see Andrea della Robbia's enamelled terracotta *Madonna and Child* on the first altar in the right aisle, and a Filippino Lippi painting of saints Jerome, Sebastian, Roch and Helen in the right transept.

Via Fillungo

This elegant street east of Piazza San Michele retains the prestige it enjoyed in the Middle Ages and Renaissance when silk merchants chose it for their imposing homes. Opposite the tower-house, Casa Barletti, the slender 13th-century Torre dell'Ore had its clock added in 1471.

Piazza Anfiteatro

Half way along Via Fillungo, this shop-lined piazza (also called del Mercato) traces the elliptical shape of the ancient Roman amphitheatre. The houses have incorporated many of its 2nd-century brick arches.

Via Guinigi

Southeast of Piazza del Mercato is the street on which the wealthy Guinigi family built their homes 53 from the early 1300s. One of the finest is the 14th-century tower-house of Michele, Francesco and Nicolao Guinigi, offering a splendid view from its battlemented top, now transformed into a miniature garden.

Museo Nazionale

Housed in the 17th-century Palazzo Manzi, Via Galli Tassi 43, the National Museum includes paintings gathered from many Italian cities. From Siena, see Beccafumi's *Scipio* and Sodoma's *Christ Bearing the Cross*; from Florence, Pontormo's *Portrait of a Youth* and Bronzino's Medici dukes *Cosimo I* and *Ferdinando I*; from Venice, Jacopo Bassano's *Adoration of the Shepherds* and Tintoretto's *Portrait of a Man*.

Museo Nazionale Guinigi

In the 15th-century Villa Guinigi, the museum is devoted to sculptural antiquities of Etruscan and Roman origin and medieval sculptures from the town's churches.

Montecatini Terme

This still fashionable spa town was made internationally famous by scenes from Federico Fellini's film *8½*.

Around the Parco delle Terme, take the waters for digestion, liver or respiratory ailments at the monumental baths of the Art Nouveau Excelsior, the neo-classical Leopoldini or the Grecian-colonnaded Tettuccio. Or join the ghost of Marcello Mastroianni with a strong brandy at the Grand Hotel e la Pace, a Belle Epoque pile south of the park on Via della Torretta.

Collodi

The hill town just 13 km (8 miles) west of Montecatini is best known for its theme park, Parco di Pinocchio. The long-nosed puppet was created by journalist Carlo Collodi who adopted his mother's birthplace as his pen-name.

Adults will enjoy the lovely 18th-century gardens of the Villa Garzoni.

Pistoia

The now largely modern town, famous for its centuries-old fruit and vegetable markets, has an attractive *centro storico* around Piazza del Duomo.

The art treasures of the Pisan-Romanesque cathedral include a Coppo di Marcovaldo *Crucifixion* (1274) in the right aisle, preceding a chapel with the great silver *Dossale di San Jacopo* (St James Altar, 13th–15th centuries). This has 628 biblical figures by Tuscan artists.

Opposite the cathedral is Andrea Pisano's octagonal Gothic

baptistery with a fine polychrome font (1226). The otherwise unassuming little 12th-century church of Sant' Andrea can claim the town's most valued work of art in Giovanni Pisano's masterpiece, the magnificently sculpted marble pulpit (1301).

Prato

Textiles, principally wool, continue to make this town's fortune, and pilgrims come to see the legendary relic of a girdle that Mary gave to Doubting Thomas. It is housed in Santo Stefano cathedral and displayed five times a year from the cathedral's 15th-century exterior pulpit, Pergamo del Sagro Cingolo (Holy Girdle). The pulpit was designed by Michelozzo, and its balustrade is decorated with superb sculpted reliefs by Donatello (the originals are now in the cathedral museum to the left of the church). In the choir, Fra Filippo Lippi's frescoes (1466) of John the Baptist and St Stephen are regarded as the maverick monk's masterpieces. More of his work can be seen in the Galleria Comunale over in the Gothic Palazzo Pretorio, along with Bernardo Daddi's 14th-century polyptych of the Holy Girdle story. South of the Duomo, the Renaissance church of Santa Maria delle Carceri is a late 15th-century work by Giuliano da Sangallo.

Vinci

In the 13th-century Castello dei Conti Guidi, the town celebrates its most famous son Leonardo at the Museo Leonardiano. Besides facsimiles of preparatory drawings for his paintings, this delightful museum displays some models and documents of the genius's scientific inventions, including machines for bridge-building, flying and machine-tools.

Baby Leonardo is believed to have been baptised in the font of the village church of Santa Croce. He was actually born up the hill in the hamlet of Anchiana.

Empoli

Glass is a major industry here and Chianti wine bottles can be seen manufactured at the glassworks on Piazza Gramsci. The Romanesque Collegiata di Sant'Andrea has a green and white marble façade with a porch added in the 16th century. Since the heavy World War II bombardment, its art works are now displayed in the modern museum next door, notably Masolino's *Pietà* fresco (1425) and Lorenzo di Monaco's *Madonna of Humility* (1404).

At the 14th-century Santo Stefano degli Agostiniani, it was not bombs but revolutionaries who damaged the Masolini frescoes in 1792, now painstakingly restored in fragmentary form.

It was from Tuscany's southwest corner that the Etruscan and ancient Roman merchant ships set off around the Mediterranean—from Argentario, Talamone, Populonia and the island of Elba. The coast is now a popular resort area for modern Romans. Inland, the Maremma has been turned into a nature reserve and Massa Marittima attracts art-lovers to its cathedral and museums.

Orbetello

It stands on a sand and rock embankment, one of three linking the mainland to the Argentario peninsula and its sailing harbours. Orbetello is one of Tuscany's most ancient towns, with traces of a late Villanovan necropolis (9th century BC). The parade of invaders ever since is a miniature history of Tuscany itself—Etruscans, Romans, Byzantines, Lombards, Sienese, Spaniards, French and Austrians.

World War II bombardment has left only a few monuments. From the Spanish era, the 16th-century Porta Nuova; the porticoed Viceroy's Palace (il Padiglione) on Piazza Garibaldi and, southeast of the city centre, the powder-house (Polveriera Guzman). Only the Gothic portal of the cathedral dates from its reconstruction in 1376, on the site of an ancient pagan temple.

Orbetello Lagoon

The northern half of the salt-water lagoon formed by the embankments is protected by the WWF as a nature reserve for its classical Mediterranean landscape of scrubby underbrush and a bird sanctuary for flamingos and spoonbills.

Argentario

A scenic route runs 40 km (25 miles) around the fist-shaped peninsula past clifftop Spanish watch-towers—with porcupines creeping across the road. Orange and lemon trees, olive groves and vineyards adorn the slopes of Monte Argentario. Nightingales, peregrine falcons and wild boar make their home in the oak and pine woods higher up towards the summit, at 635 m (2083 ft).

Porto Ercole

The fashionable resort's sailing harbour has long been popular

Animals peer out from a forest of columns in Massa Marittima's cathedral.

ARGENTARIO • MAREMMA NATURE RESERVE

with royals, near-royals and lesser mortals, the merely well-heeled yachting fraternity.

A plaque on the gateway-entrance to town honours the great painter Caravaggio, who died on the beach here in 1610 and is believed to have been buried anonymously in Sant' Erasmo parish church. The port has a lively early-morning fish market and a more relaxed atmosphere later on in its quayside cafés and seafood restaurants. Restored after wartime bombardment, the Spanish fortifications—La Rocca and the Santa Barbara and Santa Caterina bastions—have been transformed into private apartments.

Porto Santo Stefano

The larger of Argentario's two ports is now thoroughly modern but is distinguished by a great fish market. The harbour offers boat cruises to explore the peninsula and outlying isles of Giglio and Giannutri.

Maremma Nature Reserve

The fishing village of Talamone, originally an important Etruscan port-town, is the southern gateway to the Parco Naturale della Maremma. Overlooking the harbour, the 15th-century Rocca castle's Natural History Museum provides a well-documented introduction to the nature reserve (as well as finds from Etruscan and Roman antiquity).

On a narrow coastal strip, the nature reserve extends 15 km (9 miles) north to the mouth of the Ombrone river, in a classical Mediterranean landscape of heath, marsh and woodland of elm, pine, strawberry-tree, oak and holly oak. East of the estuary, midget palms grow on the unspoiled beaches at Marina di Alberese. *Butteri* (cowboys) herd the long-horned cattle and the Maremma's famous horses for an August rodeo at Alberese, the northern entrance to the park.

Garden of the Tarots

At Garavicchio near Capalbio, the French artist Niki de Sainte-Phalle created a colourful sculpture garden, open in summer.

HIGHLIGHTS

- **Argentario**: peninsula's fashionable resorts of Porto Ercole and Porto Santo Stefano
- **Maremma**: nature reserve
- **Massa Marittima**: great Romanesque-Gothic cathedral
- **Elba**: Napoleon's palazzo and villa, Portoferraio's old harbour

Grossetto

The town has become an important centre for agricultural production thanks to the Maremma swamp-drying and land-reclamation programme started 350 years ago by the Dukes of Tuscany. Today, the city has taken on a modern face around the small *centro storico*. The formidable Fortezza Medicea (Medici fortress) still stands, while bastions along the hexagonal ramparts have been transformed into public gardens.

On Piazza Indipendenza, the 13th-century Gothic church of San Francesco prizes the high altar *Crucifixion* (1289) by Duccio di Buoninsegna and a fine Renaissance well in the cloister. The 13th-century cathedral on Piazza Dante now has a 19th-century neo-Romanesque red and white marble façade. In the left transept, the Madonna delle Grazie altar has a splendid *Assumption* (1474) by Matteo di Giovanni.

The Archaeological Museum, Piazza Baccarini, includes in its collection of Etruscan and Roman antiquities a noteworthy bust of Emperor Hadrian.

Beaches

Surrounded by pine trees, the town's beach, Marina di Grosseto, is a short drive west. North along the coast, Castiglione della Pescaia has a good sailing and fishing harbour and very popular beaches. Further north, the luxury resort of Punta Ala has stretches of sand sheltered by dense pine groves, as well as polo, golf and yachting.

Follonica

Crowded from spring to early autumn, the town's sandy beaches lie at the centre of the curving Gulf of Follonica. Back from the coast, the factory town began over 2,000 years ago with Etruscan foundries working iron ore from Elba. Under the Medici, it enjoyed a monopoly of cannonball manufacture. To trace this history, an Iron Museum *(Museo del Ferro)* has been installed in San Ferdinando foundry.

Local artists are exhibited at the Civica Pinacoteca museum in the 1920s Casa del Popolo on Via Roma.

Massa Marittima

Less than 20 km (12 miles) northeast of Follonica, the city boasts one of Tuscany's most handsome cathedrals, a jewel of Romanesque-Gothic architecture in the Pisan style. This and other art treasures were financed by riches amassed from silver and copper mining in the surrounding hills.

Rising majestically on a platform at the southwest corner of the *centro storico*, the 13th-cen-

Porto Ercole's sheltered harbour is a favourite with Romans and royalty.

tury Duomo has a rectangular campanile set back from the basilica. The dome over the chancel was added in the 15th century. In the interior, the columns have finely carved floral and animal motifs on the capitals. Immediately left of the entrance is a 14th-century Sienese *Madonna and Child*. Over to the right, the bas-reliefs on the baptismal fonts (carved in 1267 from one massive travertine block) portray the life of John the Baptist. Behind the high altar is the grand Gothic tomb (1324) of the town's 6th-century patron saint Cerbone. In the Cappella della Madonna (left transept), the altar-painting has scenes of the *Passion* and *Crucifixion* attributed to the school of Duccio di Buoninsegna.

Opposite the cathedral, in the 13th-century Palazzo del Podestà, the Museo Civico exhibits both Etruscan antiquities and a collection of 14th- and 15th-century Sienese painting. Highlights are Sassetta's *Archangel Gabriel* and Ambrogio Lorenzetti's *Maestà*.

Elba

This island of Napoleon Bonaparte's exile is now a great place for water sports—snorkelling, wind-surfing, sailing, fishing in its clear waters—and for excursions into its rugged interior.

The island, 27 km (17 miles) long and 5 km (3 miles) wide, was mined by the Etruscans for its iron. The deposits remained rich enough to furnish the dukes of Tuscany with raw material for their armaments, and continue to be mined today at Rio Marina.

Portoferraio

The modern ferry dock is the principal port of entry for traffic from the mainland port of Piombino. The old harbour of "Iron Port" founded by Duke Cosimo I de' Medici in 1548 is reserved for smaller craft and fishing boats. The fortified Porta a Mare gate (1637) leads to the *centro storico*. The main square is Piazza della Repubblica, with the 17th-century cathedral and Palazzo comunale, also known as the Biscotteria since its ovens were used for the military garrison's bread. The Fortezza Linguella houses an archaeological museum of Etruscan and Roman antiquities. The most important of the Medici fortifications is the massive Forte del Falcone northwest of town.

Napoleon's Villas

Napoleon Bonaparte, for whom Elba was the extent of his empire from June 1814 till he escaped in February 1815, had two homes here, collectively the Museo nazionale delle Residenze napoleoniche. Accessible from Piazza della Repubblica on the heights above Portoferraio, his townhouse is a villa knocked together from two windmills, Palazzina dei Mulini. With the apartment of his sister Pauline, the Emperor's rooms today contain furniture of the period and books from his Fontainebleau library. The servants' quarters display a collection of Italian, French and German anti-Napoleon caricatures.

In the hills southwest of Portoferraio, the summer residence Villa San Martino is decorated with Vincenzo Revelli's fanciful frescoes of the Egyptian campaign in 1798.

Around the Island

On the south coast, Marina di Campo is a popular resort with first-class water sports facilities. Fetovaia has more secluded beaches in the southwest corner. On the north coast, resorts on Bidola and Procchio bays offer fine sandy beaches and good hotels. In the fishing village of Marciana Marina, the fragrance of oleander and magnolia prevails over that of freshly caught sardines in the harbour. Up in the hills, Marciana Alta is a charming medieval village with an archaeological museum for prehistoric and Etruscan artefacts and ceramics. For a view over the whole island, take the cable car to the top of Monte Capanne, 1,019 m (3343 ft).

Ancient Arezzo is a provincial capital with magnificent art treasures and a jousting tournament that makes a worthy counterpart to Siena's *Palio*. Both there and amid the rolling landscapes of the upper Tiber valley where he grew up, the great Renaissance painter Piero della Francesca created many of his finest masterpieces. To the north, the Arno rises in the wild and densely wooded Casentino hills. In the sunny south is the old Etruscan town of Cortona.

Arezzo

With a settlement here since the Stone Age, Arezzo has preferred historically to play it safe. One of the 12 cities of the Etruscan Federation, it soon became a faithful ally of conquering Rome. In 1336, it abandoned support of the German emperor's Ghibellines to surrender to Florence's papal Guelphs. Merchants profited from Florentine protection to finance the town's grand churches and palazzi, some of the finest in Tuscany. Poet Petrarch and libertine humanist Pietro Aretino were born here, as was Giorgio Vasari, pioneering art historian of the Renaissance and a painter and architect in his own right. Today, the town has diversified beyond its traditional activity as a distribution centre for agricultural produce, to bring in significant revenue as an international centre for the goldsmith's trade.

Church of San Francesco

Behind its rough-hewn, unfinished façade, this 14th-century church shelters an art treasure attracting pilgrimages from all over the world equal to any drawn by the holiest of religious relics. Piero della Francesca's *True Cross* fresco cycle is an undisputed summit of Renaissance painting. In the church standing at the centre of the old town west of the Piazza Grande, Piero's brilliantly restored frescoes (1452–66) adorn the choir beyond the main altar. In ten scenes, the medieval legend of the Cross incorporates biblical elements from the death of Adam to King Solomon and the Queen of Sheba, and the 4th-century quest of Emperor Constantine's mother Helena to find the Cross buried in Jerusalem. Piero's mathematic mastery of perspective and colour draws on his poetic sense of human

Full of charm, Cortona looks out over the Chiana valley.

values to convey both grand pageant and personal intimacy. The Gothic church's plain but bright interior benefits from the 16th-century stained-glass windows of French-born Guillaume de Marcillat—to the Italians, Guglielmo di Marcillat.

Piazza Grande

The dramatically sloping main square, setting of Roberto Benigni's Oscar-winning film, *La Vita è bella*, is surrounded by handsome 16th- and 17th-century palazzi and the apse and campanile of the parish church.

At the top of the slope, enjoy the view in a café and restaurant beneath the portico of the elongated Palazzo delle Logge, designed by Giorgio Vasari. On the west side, the Palazzo della Fraternità dei Laici is a fine combination of Gothic and Renaissance architecture with Bernardo Rossellino's colonnaded loggia surmounted by a bell-tower. The adjacent Palazzo del Tribunale has a severity appropriate to the town's courthouse.

In early September (and in the summer), Piazza Grande stages the spectacular Giostra del Saracino (Saracen's Joust), preceded by festive pageantry. In Renaissance costume, eight horsemen, two from each of Arezzo's four historic quarters, ride full tilt across the square to thrust their lance at a Saracen figure which may whirl round and cudgel an unwary rider off his horse.

Pieve di Santa Maria

The façade of the 12th-century Romanesque parish church (on Corso Italia) has a colonnade similar to those in Lucca and Pisa. Pillars in the transitional Gothic interior have some finely sculpted capitals. In the presbytery, see Pietro Lorenzetti's polyptych (1320) with an *Annunciation* and *Madonna and Child*.

Duomo

In 1914 the present neo-Gothic façade was added to the cathedral, but the largely 16th-century interior is worth a visit for another great fresco by Piero della Francesca, *Mary Magdalen*, at the entrance to the sacristy.

Passeggio del Prato

North of Piazza Grande, this delightful park offers shady pine trees and lawns for a siesta or picnic with a fine view of the surrounding country. The massive 16th-century Fortezza Medicea stands at the eastern edge of the park. More soothing is the monument (1928) to Arezzo's 14th-century poet Petrarch. His house, just south of the park at Via dell' Orto 28, displays the poet's memorabilia.

Museo d'Arte Medievale e Moderna

In the 15th-century Palazzo Bruni Ciocchi, Via San Lorentino 8, the museum exhibits a collection of Tuscan art from the 13th to 19th centuries. Notable are works by Rossellino, Signorelli, Vasari and Rosso Fiorentino. There is also a beautiful collection of majolica ceramics from Islamic Spain, Gubbio, Faenza and Pesaro.

Museo Archeologico Mecenate

At Via Margaritone 10, the archaeological museum is housed in the 14th-century monastery of San Bernardo built along the curve of the Roman amphitheatre (separate entrance Via Crispi 50). The collection's highlights include Arezzo's celebrated Etruscan red-figure pottery along with Etruscan and Roman bronzes, ceramics and glassware.

Museo Vasariano

The 16th-century house of Giorgio Vasari, Via XX Settembre 55, was built by the Arezzo-born architect and is now a museum. It is decorated with his own allegorical frescoes, other paintings and his original scale model in wood for the Palazzo delle Logge.

Monterchi

Surrounded by vineyards and orchards, this pretty hilltop village lies 30 km (18 miles) east of Arezzo at the heart of the upper Tiber valley country in which Piero della Francesca grew up. His mother's birthplace has a unique fresco that is seen as the artist's sublime homage to her. The *Madonna del Parto* (1455) is a rare portrayal of the Virgin Mary in pregnancy. It depicts a Mary of noble and rustic simplicity to whom country girls have come over the centuries to seek a blessing for their own unborn babies. It is currently displayed in a special room in the local elementary school, pending its return to the Santa Maria in Momentana Chapel, near the cemetery where Piero's mother is believed to be buried.

Anghiari

The fortified farm town 12 km (7 miles) north of Monterchi is best known for having presided in 1440 over a great Florentine victory over Milan in the plain below. Piero della Francesca is believed to have used his own eye-witness drawings for a battle scene in his Arezzo fresco cycle.

The medieval town walls are well preserved, offering stark contrast to the 19th-century steel-and-glass Galleria Magi arcade on Piazza Baldaccio.

At the top of the steeply sloping Via Trieste, the 18th-century church of Santa Maria delle Grazie has, to the right of its high altar, a rare polychrome wooden *Madonna* (1316) by Tino di Camaino and a *Madonna, Saints and Angels* by Matteo di Giovanni. On the lower Piazza Mameli, the Renaissance Palazzo Tagli-eschi houses the regional museum devoted to art of the upper Tiber Valley, notably a Jacopo della Quercia *Madonna* in polychrome wood.

Sansepolcro

Piero della Francesco's birthplace, 8 km (5 miles) east of Anghiari, has retained in its centro storico many of the Gothic buildings the artists grew up with in the 15th century.

Via Matteotti has characteristic medieval and Renaissance tower-houses, such as the twin-towered Palazzo Gherardi and Palazzo Pichi-Sermoli.

Arezzo's Pieve di Santa Maria—its belltower "of a hundred holes" is the symbol of the city.

Duomo

Restored in the 20th century, the cathedral has preserved its handsome Romanesque-Gothic interior. In the sanctuary is the *Resurrection* polyptych by Niccolò di Segna, which Piero saw and studied before treating the same subject. His version is now in the Museo Civico.

Museo Civico

Housed in the 14th-century Gothic Palazzo dei Conservatori, Via Aggiunti 65, the museum has three of Piero della Francesca's acknowledged masterpieces: the *Resurrection* (1463); a *Madonna della Misericordia* polyptych (1460); *San Giuliano*; while *San Ludovico* is attributed to his disciple Lorentino. There are also important works by Matteo di Giovanni, Luca Signorelli and Pontormo.

Casentino

A day trip into the beautiful Casentino hills of the upper Arno valley, starting just 30 km (18 miles) north of Arezzo, may at first seem like an excursion into an idyllic but uncannily "un-Italian" region of northern Europe. Dense woodland of silver fir and beech replace the more familiar Tuscan olive groves, vineyards and cypresses. Castle ruins on remote crags are last reminders of medieval battles between the Guelphs and Ghibellines—the bloodiest being at Campaldino, just outside Poppi, in 1289.

Bibbiena

The Casentino's main town is an important agricultural centre, once the fief of the Tarlati lords. Two battlemented towers remain from their feudal castle on Piazza Tarlati, with a terrace from which to survey the valley. The 12th-century family chapel is now the parish church, with a strange *Annunciation* (1585) in the right transept and a Biccio di Lorenzo *Madonna and Saints* triptych on the high altar.

Poppi

This fine old fortified town somehow preserves a medieval atmosphere along its narrow porticoed streets as they climb to the formidable hilltop Palazzo Pretorio. Master builder Arnolfo di Cambio worked as apprentice on this 13th-century civic stronghold and may have used it as a model for Florence's Palazzo Vecchio. It has an elegant inner courtyard and Taddeo Gaddi's frescoes in its top-floor chapel.

Romena

Overlooking the western slopes of the Arno valley and visible from afar are three remaining towers (originally 14) of the Guidi lords' grand 11th-century

Castello di Romena, which provided refuge for Dante in 1300 after he fled from Florence. See, too, a little further down, the 12th-century Romanesque parish church, San Pietro di Romena.

Camàldoli National Park

The park embraces a vast forest and Monte Falterona, 1,654 m (5,427 ft), on which the Arno takes its source. Beside the predominant silver fir and beech, the trees include poplar, sycamore, oak, chestnut, birch and alder.

A mountain road winds 20 km (12 miles) east from Poppi up into the middle of the forest where monks founded the Camàldoli Hermitage (Eremo) in 1012. A dozen monks still live there, worshipping at an 18th-century baroque church. To the south is the 16th-century Fontebuono Monastery. Only its pharmacy is open to the public, dispensing herbal medicines and potent liqueurs.

Cortona

Tucked away in its southeastern corner, one of Tuscany's most enchanting towns often seems in a world of its own, reclining peacefully on a ridge surrounded by olive groves and vineyards. On the way up, visit the 15th-century Santa Maria delle Grazie al Calcinaio, a Renaissance greystone church of admirable simplicity with stained-glass rose-

windows by Guillaume de Marcillat. Climbing to the *centro storico*, steep, narrow streets open out onto vistas of the Chiana valley to the west and Umbria's Lake Trasimeno to the south.

The walls of the largely medieval town retain traces of its Etruscan foundation in the 4th century BC, most visible at the ancient Porta Colonia on the northern perimeter.

Piazza Repubblica and Piazza Signorelli

City life is centred around these two adjacent squares. In the 13th-century Palazzo Casali here, the Museo dell'Accademia Etrusca possesses one of Italy's most important collections of Etruscan and Roman antiquities. A highlight among the bronzes is the 16-lamp chandelier (5th century BC), along with figures of animals and warriors. A small collection of paintings includes works by Cortona-born Luca Signorelli and a major *Madonna* altar painting (1628) by Pietro da Cortona.

Museo Diocesano

Housed in the old church of Gesù opposite the cathedral, the museum has a first-rate collection of Tuscan masters, including Pietro Lorenzetti's *Crucifixion* and *Enthroned Madonna*, Fra Angelico's *Annunciation*; and Luca Signorelli's *Deposition*.

◼▶ A WEEKEND IN UMBRIA

Lake Trasimeno, Perugia, Gubbio, Assisi

The green and pleasant province of Umbria offers an agreeable weekend excursion from southern Tuscany. Starting out, for instance, from Montepulciano or Cortona, you can make a comfortable triangular tour via the lovely Lake Trasimeno to the lively university town of Perugia, hilltop Gubbio—a medieval city famous for its ceramics—to end up in Assisi, pilgrimage town of St Francis.

Midway between Florence and Rome, the region was largely dominated by the papacy from the Middle Ages until Italy's unification in the 19th century. Papal patronage left its mark on its wealth of art treasures.

Lake Trasimeno

Some 45 km (28 miles) in circumference, the lake has swimming beaches at Tuoro (near the battlefield of Hannibal's famous victory over the Romans in 217 BC). From Passignano you can take a boat cruise out to Isola Maggiore. St Francis of Assisi made the trip in 1211, an event marked by two chapels on the island. Birdwatchers may still spot some of the saint's favourite birds: eagle owl, osprey, stork, egret, whooper swan and crested grebe.

Perugia

Two universities, Italian and international, give the town a cosmopolitan atmosphere. Its hilltop position at 494 m (1620 ft) commands good views of the rolling Umbrian countryside.

Set in the medieval ramparts on the north side of the *centro storico*, the Arco Etrusco, a triumphal arch part Etruscan and part Roman, attests to the city's ancient past—and perennial conflicts with neighbouring Assisi.

Fontana Maggiore

In the town's main square, Piazza IV Novembre, is Nicola and Giovanni Pisano's beautifully carved fountain (1278) formed by two concentric polygonal basins. Bas-reliefs on the lower basin depict the farmers' annual labours, signs of the Zodiac and the seven liberal arts. The upper basin's reliefs portray Perugia's legendary foundation.

Palazzo dei Priori

Rising proudly above the piazza, the towering Gothic town hall completed in 1443 is a magnificent assertion of civic pride. But notice, too, the elegance of the façade's triple mullioned windows over the monumental main portal (1346).

Galleria nazionale dell'Umbria

On the town hall's third floor is a superb collection of Umbrian and Tuscan painting. Among many paintings by the city's beloved Perugino (1445–1523) is the delicate *Sant'Agostino* polyptych. His pupil Pinturicchio has an impressive *Santa Maria dei Fossi* altar painting. Other outstanding works are Duccio di Buoninsegna's *Madonna and Child*, Fra Angelico's *San Domenico* polyptych, Piero della Francesca's *Annunciation* and *Madonna with Angels* and five sculptures (1281) by Arnolfo di Cambio.

Collegio del Cambio

On Corso Vannucci (Pietro Vannucci was Perugino's real name), is the bankers' guild 15th-century hall and chapel with an attractive set of Perugino frescoes in the Audience Hall *(Sala dell'Udienza)*. Opposite a series of religious themes, the allegorical frescoes depict the bankers' well known virtues of *Temperance*, *Prudence*, *Justice* and *Fortitude* (the latter attributed to Perugino's 17-year-old pupil Raphael).

Carducci Gardens

Relax in the gardens at the south end of Corso Vannucci with a view over the Tiber valley. An antique fair is held here on Sunday mornings.

Gubbio

Just 40 km (25 miles) north of Perugia, the timeless atmosphere and quiet, unspoiled beauty of this out-of-the-way fortified hill town rewards those who take the trouble to find it and climb its steep cobbled streets.

The stone-and-brick paved Piazza della Signoria offers a fine view over the city. One of Italy's grandest civic buildings, the fortress-like 14th-century Palazzo dei Consoli is anchored to the hillside by a lofty arcade from which to look out on the Umbrian countryside. An upstairs art gallery *(Pinacoteca)* exhibits examples of Gubbio's renowned ceramics from the 16th to 19th centuries and the paintings of local artists.

Further uphill is the splendid Renaissance Palazzo Ducale built in 1480 for Federico da Montefeltro, Urbino's powerful soldier-duke and patron of the arts.

Assisi

The fact that St Francis, the most popular saint of the Catholic Church, was born here has made this town a place of pilgrimage second in importance only to Rome itself. Recovering from the terrible earthquake of 1997, the basilica, like the medieval *centro storico*, was painstakingly restored for the Jubilee year of 2000.

Basilica di San Francesco

The basilica consists of an upper and lower church built over the crypt containing the saint's tomb (concealed from robbers until rediscovered in 1818). Begun in 1228, the Lower Church now has a Renaissance porch in front of the Gothic side entrance. The softly lit low-vaulted interior was frescoed in the 14th century—by Simone Martini for the St Martin Chapel, first left, and Giotto and his pupils for the Mary Magdalen Chapel, third right. In the right transept, Cimabue has portrayed St Francis to the right of the enthroned Madonna. In the left transept is Pietro Lorenzetti's *Descent from the Cross*.

The Upper Church interior offers a stark, brilliantly lit contrast. Beginning in the transept, Cimabue's frescoes have badly deteriorated, but the *Crucifixion* still has powerful emotion. In the nave, scholars agree that Giotto did preside over if not execute the series of 28 frescoes (1296–1300) depicting the *Life of St Francis*.

Centro Storico

"Via Superba" in the Middle Ages, Via San Francesco leads to the heart of old Assisi. The 17th-century Palazzo Bernabei, No. 19A, houses part of Perugia University. The 15th-century Oratorio dei Pellegrini (Pilgrims), No. 11, has frescoes attributed to Perugino. Piazza del Comune, surrounded by medieval palazzi, stands on the site of the Roman Forum. Epitomizing Christianity's victory over Roman paganism, the church of Santa Maria sopra Minerva was a Roman temple in the 1st century AD.

FRANCIS OF ASSISI (1182–1226)

Like many a holy man before him, Giovanni di Bernardone found his way to sanctity from a life of decadent riches. Starting out as a wealthy young hooligan, he fell critically ill after a spell in a Perugia jail at 23. A vision in the Chapel of San Damiano moved him to a vow of poverty in the service of the Church, caring for lepers and reforming bandits. He learned the ills of the world in Spain, Morocco, Egypt and Palestine and returned home to preach love and peace in an Italy torn by strife. Thousands flocked to his sermons and told how his gentle manner had tamed wild beasts and taught birds to sing more sweetly. At a retreat on Monte La Verna, near Arezzo, his religious ecstasy brought the marks of Christ's stigmata—which even the most sceptical scholars have not questioned. In 1228, just two years after his death, he was canonized St Francis.

Art and Architecture

The specific character of Tuscan art has always reflected the charm of the landscape and the power of Tuscany's princes and merchants. Grace and dignity infused the art of the Etruscans, the painting of Siena, the architecture of Pisa and the whole panoply of creativity in Renaissance Florence.

Beginnings

The essential Tuscan taste for the good life can already be seen in the simply decorated Villanovan ceramics of the earliest known settlers. These refugees from Central Europe gave their clay pots a deep ruddy sheen to imitate the precious bronze they needed for their handsome war-helmets (1100 BC).

Etruscan Art

From the 8th century BC, the opulent art of the Etruscans expressed a new prosperity. Perhaps Asiatic rather than European in origin, their taste for the exotic was in stark contrast to the art of their Greek contemporaries and the Romans who came after.

Etruscan tombs, practically the sole surviving examples of their architecture, were stylized ver-

The public baths at Fiesole were built during the rule of Hadrian.

sions of their living rooms, apparently a modest rectangular chamber with a double sloping ceiling divided by a long cylindrical beam. Their superb talents as goldsmiths can be seen in the tomb-treasure in the museums of Florence, Volterra, Siena, Arezzo, Chiusi and Cortona: jewellery and ornaments in granulated patterns, delicately chased or decorated with fine engraving and lacy filigree. Ivory from Ethiopia and Egypt is treated with equal refinement, carved for statuettes, plaques for funerary caskets and handles for mirrors.

Their fine black *bucchero* pottery is a sophisticated imitation of precious metals. Trade with Greece in the 8th and 7th centuries BC had a limited effect on Etruscan ceramics. But they showed a much stronger affinity with what were perhaps their cousins in Anatolia or Phoenicia in the motifs on their vases and jewellery: bizarre sphinxes, griffins and other monsters. By the 6th century BC, Etruscan creativity succumbed to Greek cultural imperialism, and Tuscany was flooded with cheap imitations of mass-produced Corinthian or Attic vases.

In painting, the richly coloured frescoes of Chiusi tell us less about Etruscan art than about the Greek styles they imitated in the 5th century BC (vanished from Greece itself). Sculpture digests Greek influences without sacrificing Etruscan originality and individualism. The lion-like *Chimera*, one of the great bronze statues of all antiquity (5th century BC, Florence's archaeological museum), has a stunning energy. Bronze death masks or portraits painted on the coffin lid remain highly personal. In later stone sculptures covering the sarcophagus, the deceased man is frequently shown reclining with his spouse, as if attending a banquet with the gods. The simple realism of the *Obese Etruscan* (2nd century BC) seeks neither the Greeks' idealized beauty nor gratuitous ugliness.

The Romans

Rome built little of artistic importance in Tuscany. However, the countless hills of this minor colonial outpost did at least provide a good testing ground for Roman road-building. Architecturally,

Fiesole's amphitheatre seating 3,000 spectators is the major achievement, along with a temple, also of the 1st century BC, incorporating elements of an earlier Etruscan sanctuary. A good example of brick arches can be seen in the nearby public baths built under Emperor Hadrian in the 1st century AD.

Romanesque Architecture

Two separate traditions developed in Romanesque architecture, because Pisa's flourishing maritime empire kept it independent of Florence from the 11th to the 13th centuries. With a façade of tiered arcades above three porches, Pisa's cathedral (begun in 1063) set a dominant style. Arab, Byzantine and Armenian decorative elements were introduced by architect Buschetto (c.1050–c.1110), who gathered them on his visits to the eastern Mediterranean.

Pisa's juxtaposition of cathedral with baptistery, free-standing Leaning Tower *(campanile)* and burial ground *(camposanto)* are decidedly theatrical, but even more so is the cathedral of Massa Marittima, posed on a podium. The decorative arcaded façades pop up again in Lucca, Pistoia and way over in Arezzo.

Florence sets its own standards with the Basilica of San Miniato (largely 12th century). In its geo-

The Italian taste for architectural "stage sets" found its earliest expression in Pisa.

metrically patterned façade of green and white marble, the Florentines have chosen harmony of colour and clarity of line over what they would regard as the "fussy" sculptural delicacies of Pisan design. Indeed, for sheer purity of geometric forms and exquisite juxtaposition of white Carrara and green Prato marble, the cathedral's baptistery, frequently overlooked architecturally because the attention of most visitors is attracted by the Renaissance bronze doors, is the veritable jewel of Florentine Romanesque.

In the simpler forms of civic building, the communes assert their emerging pride with San Gimignano's stone towers and the town hall at Massa Marittima.

Painting
before the Renaissance

In the 13th century, Tuscan painters broke with the lethargic aesthetics which Byzantine style had imposed on Italian art. Florence-born Coppo di Marcovaldo (1225–75) brought unfamiliar intense emotion to his convulsed *Crucifixion* at San Gimignano. Cimabue (1240–1302) injected a new humanity into Byzantine formalism with his *Madonna and Child Enthroned* (Uffizi) and *Crucifixion* (Santa Croce). 75

The work of Duccio di Buoninsegna (c.1255–c.1318) respects the austere Byzantine tradition but adds an elegance and sensitivity that became the hallmark of the Siena school of painting that he founded. This can be seen both in his *Madonna Enthroned* in the Siena cathedral-museum and the *Rucellai Madonna* in the Uffizi.

But the breakthrough comes with Giotto (1267–1337). He achieves psychological and physical realism by breaking away from the stylized figures of medieval art, conferring on bodies a new depth and density, as if they were based on live models. As restorers work on saving the Assisi frescoes damaged by the earthquake of 1997, we can still admire in Florence his *Ognissanti Madonna* at the Uffizi, and the Bardi and Peruzzi Chapel frescoes in the church of Santa Croce. Also in Santa Croce you can see frescoes by his most notable pupils: Taddeo Gaddi (active 1325–66) working with subdued elegance in the Baroncelli Chapel; and Maso di Banco (active 1336–50), whose *St Sylvester* cycle in the second Bardi Chapel shows something of his master's fine plastic sense and use of intense colour.

The Sienese taste for opulent elegance is epitomized by Simone Martini (c.1284–1344) in his *Madonna Enthroned* in the town's Palazzo Pubblico, and masterful altarpieces—*St Catherine* in Pisa's San Matteo museum and an *Annunciation* in the Uffizi. His work launched the decorative International Gothic style, which he spread throughout Europe when working with the French kings of Naples and at the court of the popes exiled in Avignon. Back home, brothers Pietro and Ambrogio Lorenzetti (active 1319–48) are unique in the scope of detail with which they depict life in Siena and the surrounding countryside, both allegorical and realistic, in the Palazzo Pubblico's *Good Government* and *Bad Government*.

Sculpture:
13th and 14th centuries

In the psychological expressiveness of his pulpit for Siena cathedral, Nicola Pisano (1210–78) did for modern sculpture what Giotto was to do for painting. Long before the Renaissance masters, he drew on ancient Roman and Greek models of soldiers and mythical heroes for his saints and patriarchs. The graphic, tightly packed scenes on his pulpit for the Pisa baptistery are clearly 77

Duccio di Buoninsegna also worked on stained glass in Siena cathedral.

inspired by the marble panels of Etruscan and Roman sarcophagi.

His son Giovanni Pisano (1248–1314) collaborated with Nicola on the Siena cathedral pulpit before striking out on his own. He brought great turbulent energy to his ambitious sculpture for the façade of Siena cathedral and pulpits in Pistoia, Prato and Massa Marittima, as well as the cathedral pulpit at Pisa.

Andrea Pisano (active 1290–1348) was no relative of Nicola and Giovanni but deserves recognition nevertheless for the magnificent bronze doors he designed for the Florence baptistery. Lessons learned from working with Giotto on the Campanile are evident in the beautifully observed scenes of craftsmen and scientists on panels which are too often overshadowed by the more famous work of Ghiberti on the other doors.

Gothic Architecture

Town halls vied with cathedrals in Tuscan Gothic architecture as city fathers rivalled the princes of the church in the late 13th and 14th centuries. Florence seated its government in the solid fortress of the Palazzo Vecchio (1298) designed by Arnolfo di Cambio to confront enemies with battlements, menacing tower and minimum space for windows. The police chief's equally formidable Bargello residence made an admirable prison. A slender tower makes Siena's Palazzo Pubblico (1297) less aggressive. With the harmonious design of its private palazzi, the Campo became the model for city squares in southern Tuscany—Volterra, Arezzo and Montepulciano.

Designed by Giovanni Pisano, Siena's cathedral (1284) is the greatest of Tuscany's Gothic churches. Its grand polychrome marble façade affirms the Italian pictorial tradition, avoiding the purely architectural effects of French or German Gothic. In Florence, Santa Maria Novella (1279) and Santa Croce (1294) in no way emulate north European Gothic's elaborate lofty stone cages, replacing walls with spacious arcades and monumental stained glass windows. Italians wanted plenty of good wall space for side-aisle paintings and chapel frescoes. Similarly, the Orsanmichele (1377) oratory may be Gothic in its triple-mullioned windows, but it is above all a showcase for the city's sculptors, as is the Loggia dei Lanzi (begun 1376). Though begun in 1294 by Arnolfo di Cambio, Florence's hybrid, largely neo-Gothic cathedral was completed only in 1887, sad company for Giotto's campanile, regarded by many as Italy's finest single Gothic monument.

Renaissance Sculpture: 15th Century

The astounding explosion of sculptural genius in Florence at the beginning of the 15th century is due in no small part to the money made available for it by the city's wealthy merchants. The baptistery competition they announced in 1401 for designing two bronze doors to go with Andrea Pisano's attracted such masters as Brunelleschi, Ghiberti and Jacopo della Quercia. Winner Lorenzo Ghiberti (1378–1455) could pay Donatello and Uccello as his assistants and work on the doors for the next 20 years. The result displays the finesse of the goldsmith and the heroic sweep of classical antiquity.

However, Donatello (c.1386–1466) may claim to be the greatest of early Renaissance sculptors, combining innate grace and elegance with supreme technical skills and versatility. His repertory is inexhaustible: the anguish of his marble *Abraham and Isaac* and wooden *Mary Magdalene* in the cathedral museum and, all in bronze, the androgynous naked impudence of his *David* in the Bargello, the impeccably designed pulpit in San Lorenzo or his panels for the Siena baptistery.

Trained as a goldsmith, Lucca della Robbia (1400–82) achieved consummate mastery in polychrome glazed terracotta sculpture. Fine examples are his *Resurrection* and *Ascension* in Florence cathedral and some of the panels on Giotto's campanile. The workshop achieved enormous popularity under his nephew Andrea (1435–1525).

Sculpture: 16th century

It was as a sculptor that Michelangelo Buonarroti (1475–1564) wanted to be remembered, despite his achievements in architecture, painting and poetry. He was convinced his tireless quest for spiritual and heroic grandeur demanded the marble of Carrara as its medium. Though working mainly in Rome, most of the sculpture is to be seen in his native Florence, the city which formed his genius. In the Accademia gallery are the original of his *David* (1504), classical symbol of the Florentine Republic, and four struggling *Slaves* (1534) intended for the tomb of Pope Julius II. For the Medici Chapel in San Lorenzo, he sculpted the monumental tombs of Giuliano and Lorenzo, Duke of Urbino, with the allegorical figures of *Day, Night, Dawn* and *Dusk*.

Better known for his autobiography, Benvenuto Cellini (1500–71) was a superbly talented sculptor and goldsmith. His masterly metalworking technique is evident in the brilliant bronze *Per-*

seus in the Loggia dei Lanzi, while in the Bargello, you see his bravura in the bronze bust of *Duke Cosimo I.*

Painting: Early Renaissance

If Giotto prepared the ground, it is Masaccio (1401–28) who makes the quantum leap into the visual and psychological world of Renaissance painting, veritable dawn of art's modern era. In Florence, he draws on Donatello's work for the sculptural quality of his figures and on architect Brunelleschi for innovative geometric relationships and deepening perspectives. But it is his own personal vision that brings such powerful individual emotion to his frescoes for the Brancacci Chapel of Santa Maria del Carmine, painted with his greatly underestimated Brancacci collaborator Masolino (1383–1440). The new naturalism appears with great strength in Masaccio's *Trinity* for Santa Maria Novella and, another collaboration with Masolino, *Madonna and Child with St Anne* (Uffizi).

Siena's finest painter of the era is Sassetta (1392–1450), a bridge between the decorative International Gothic spirit of Simone Martini and the more formal Renaissance art of Florence, where the gentler Masolino touched him more than the uncompromising Masaccio.

Not intense but still admirably individualized are the narrative frescoes of Domenico Ghirlandaio (1449–94) in the Ognissanti refectory in Florence and a vivid portrait gallery of his Tornabuoni patrons in the Santa Maria Novella scenes of the Madonna's life.

Sandro Botticelli (1445–1510) owes his outstanding popularity among Renaissance painters to the exquisite lyrical quality of his work, both melancholy and joyful. He possessed a strong sense of a painting's architecture and perspective. He included his Medici masters in his *Adoration of the Magi,* and it was they who commissioned his *Birth of Venus* and *Allegory of Spring* (Uffizi).

Fra Angelico (1400–55) asserts a rare spirituality amid the prevailing secularization of Renaissance art. His *Annunciation* in the Museo di San Marco may be the most famous icon of Western Christian art. Admirable examples of his subtle perspectives and purity of colour and form at San Marco monastery are a *Deposition* in the Hospice and a *Crucifixion* in the Capitular Hall.

None of Fra Angelico's spiritual vocation is evident in Fra Filippo Lippi (1406–69). The religious paintings of this gifted but reluctant monk linked the simple, humanistic sobriety of Masaccio to a lighter, more colourful and complex spirit closer to the ele-

Masaccio's candid depiction of human figures in the frescoes of the Brancacci chapel was considered almost miraculous.

gance of Donatello's sculpture and the painting of Botticelli. Outstanding are a *Coronation of the Madonna* in the Uffizi and an *Annunciation* in San Lorenzo.

Piero della Francesca (c.1420–92) is a towering force among painters of his age, his intelligence and subtle aesthetics presenting a quintessence of the Renaissance spirit. Born in Borgo Sansepolcro in eastern Tuscany, he worked with Domenico Veneziano but stands outside the Florentine mainstream. When setting his human beings amid buildings or landscape, he achieves a timeless purity by combining an exquisite sense of colour with me-

ticulously calculated geometric perspectives. An aura of mystery surrounds his *Legend of the True Cross* frescoes in Arezzo, the grandiose *Resurrection* at Sansepolcro and *Pregnant Madonna* at Monterchi, even his portraits of *Federigo da Montefeltro* and his wife *Battista Sforza* in the Uffizi.

Paolo Uccello (1397–1475) is criticized for being more preoccupied with visual theory of perspective than artistic imagination. But this ignores the surrealistic poetry of his *Battle of San Romano* triptych (Uffizi, London National Gallery and Louvre) and lesser-known *Universal Flood* at Santa Maria Novella.

Painting: High Renaissance

Florence witnessed in the first decade of the 16th century a miraculous moment not only in Italian art, but also in the history of mankind. Suddenly, Leonardo da Vinci, Michelangelo and Raphael were all in the same town. This was no gathering of friends—Michelangelo could not stand either of his two rivals—just a concentration in Florence of the age's greatest artistic geniuses. Leonardo da Vinci (1452–1519) said: "A painter is not admirable unless he is universal"—easy for a man interested in mathematics, geography, geology, zoology, botany, engineering, optics, aviation, astronomy, town planning, music, athletics, sculpture and a little painting on the side. But it is only that universality that can begin to explain the man capable of giving his paintings their rich expression of complex composition and subtle intellectual and emotional ambiguities. His celebrated sfumato softening of contour light and shade is just the veil to that mystery. Only three of his works remain in Tuscany, an unbearably beautiful angel upstaging his master Verrocchio's *Baptism of Christ*, a wondrous *Annunciation* and the great unfinished *Adoration of the Magi* (all in the Uffizi).

With the sheer *terribilità* (awesomeness) of his personality, Michelangelo brought to his painting an incomparable heroic dimension in the classical tradition. His earliest painting is the very sculptural *Holy Family* in the Uffizi. After sketching the works of Giotto and Masaccio, he learned something of fresco technique with Ghirlandaio, but a great mural commissioned by the city government for the Palazzo Vecchio was interrupted by a call to Rome by Pope Julius II.

Compared with these two giants, the gentle Raphael (1483–1520) seems to many just a sentimental painter of pretty Madonnas. Certainly this most accessible of Renaissance artists suffers among scholarly critics for his great popularity. The more delicate side of his art may be traced to his Umbrian origins, but the years he spent in Florence, from 1504 to 1508, added a stronger note after his studies of Leonardo and Michelangelo. Besides *The Madonna of the Goldfinch* in the Uffizi, we can see his acute psychological observation in portraits—*Agnolo Doni* and *The Veiled Lady* in the Pitti Palace and *Pope Leon X* in the Uffizi.

Coinciding with Florence's transformation into a duchy, the often over-sophisticated Mannerists painted more for effect than honest emotion, forming a bridge between Renaissance and Baroque. Pontormo (1494–1557) displayed perfect technique in his skilful elongations and distortions of the human body, notably in his *Deposition* in the church of Santa Felicità. Agnolo Bronzino (1503–72), court painter to Duke Cosimo I, brought to his portraits in the Uffizi an icy refinement that exposes—probably only unconsciously—the artificiality of aristocratic life.

Siena, awakening momentarily to honour an almost surreal deformation of the decorative painting of its golden era, produced two notable exponents of Mannerism: Domenico Beccafumi (1486–1551) and Il Sodoma (1477–1549), who was a follower, but never a disciple, of Leonardo.

Renaissance Architecture

Though imperial Rome's stability and poise were the keynotes of Renaissance design, it was in 15th-century Florence, not in the ancient capital, that these qualities first developed. Filippo Brunelleschi (1377–1446) gives them a new elegance in his Foundling Hospital (Spedale degli Innocenti, designed in 1419) with its graceful arcades of slender columns. Florence cathedral's grandiose dome is considered Brunelleschi's masterpiece, but the full serenity of his work is best appreciated in Santa Croce's Pazzi Chapel (begun 1442).

Florence's great architectural theorist and town planner is Leon Battista Alberti (1404–72). His ideas of seeking a balance between utility and ornament come to fruition in his harmonious design for the Palazzo Rucellai (1446), breaking with the medieval concept of fortified redoubt. Bernardo Rossellino (1409–64) executed Alberti's plans for the Rucellai palace and followed his town-planning concepts for Pius II in the rebuilding of the pope's home town of Pienza.

Though allowing themselves a little decorative light relief in their inner courtyards, Florence's other Renaissance palaces still choose formidable fortress-like façades. The dominant model is the Palazzo Medici of Michelozzo (1396–1472), who also designed the imposing Palazzo Pubblico for Montepulciano. Later, Lorenzo the Magnificent studied Alberti's theories to evolve a gentler style for the Medici country residences. He hired Giuliano da Sangallo (1445–1516), whose masterpiece is the Villa Medici at Poggio a Caiano (1485).

As power shifted to Rome, High Renaissance design took on ever more grandiose dimensions in an extravagant architectural equivalent of Mannerist painting and sculpture. Before leaving for good, Michelangelo offered Florence two highly stylized designs, 83

but on a more intimate plane, for San Lorenzo's Medici Chapel and Laurentian Library (Biblioteca Laurenziana, 1524).

As all-round Renaissance Man —painter, architect, thinker and writer—Giorgio Vasari (1511–74) had everything it took to make him a worthy successor to Leonardo da Vinci—apart from genius. As it was, except for his history of the Renaissance itself, he is best remembered as architect of the Uffizi and the Corridor linking it across the Ponte Vecchio to the Pitti Palace.

Tuscan Art after the Renaissance

As the baroque movement triumphed in Rome, Naples and Turin, Tuscany became an artistic backwater. For a rare but noteworthy example of baroque architecture in Florence, see the church of San Gaetano (Via de' Tornabuoni), by Gherardo Silvani (1579–1673). On one of its altars is a *Martyrdom of St Laurence* by Tuscany's best-known painter of the period, Pietro da Cortona (1596–1669). Making his career mainly in Rome as a prince of high baroque painting, Cortona worked briefly in Florence in the 1640s. His allegorical

frescoes in the Pitti Palace extol the virtues of the Medici dukes with themes of Venus, Apollo, Mars, Jupiter and Saturn. The Pitti's Boboli Gardens, laid out by Bernardo Buontalenti (1536–1608), offer an ornate setting for baroque fountains and statuary.

Tuscan painters briefly recaptured national and European attention with the 19th-century movement of the Macchiaioli, so called because of their *macchia* or "blob" technique exploiting the effect of individual touches of paint. The group, meeting at Florence's Caffè Michelangelo, was active from 1855 to 1865, rebelling against the official Academic style stifling artistic creativity. Major exponents were Telemaco Signorini (1835–1901), Silvestro Lega (1826–95) and the Livorno-born Giovanni Fattori (1825–1908), all well represented at Florence's Gallery of Modern Art and Livorno municipal museum.

The most important of Tuscany's 20th-century architects is Giovanni Michelucci (1891–1991). He designed Florence's Santa Maria Novella railway station (1936) in a style that represented a rare act of resistance to the dominant bombast of Fascism. Its bold form pays tribute to the rationalist designs of Le Corbusier and Bauhaus functionalism while using marble cladding in homage to classical tradition.

Madonna and Child *by Beccafumi, in Siena's Pinacoteca.*

85

Shopping

For jewellery and fashion, the widest selection outside Florence is in the major tourist destinations. The provincial towns are excellent for craftwork and gourmet food and wines.

Craftwork

Siena is renowned for antique embroidery. Reproductions of the neighbourhoods' *Palio* banners make great wall-hangings. Prato is famous for its fabrics and Pistoia for its embroidery and knitwear. Sansepolcro still produces traditional handmade laceware.

Arezzo, known for gold and silver jewellery continues to manufacture the red Aretine pottery that made its fortune in Etruscan and Roman antiquity. Cortona produces fine copperware while Montepulciano's speciality is stone mosaics. Carrara's marble goes into cheese boards, chess boards and all manner of table ornaments. Volterra and Pisa are both known for their carved alabaster. The old mining centres of Elba and Massa Marittima are the places to buy rough-cut minerals and crystals.

Gourmet Delicacies

If you like sharp cheeses, try Pienza's *pecorino*. Montepulciano, Siena and Arezzo all make their own fine salami sausage. Among sweetmeats, try Siena's *panforte nero*, dark honey-cake with walnuts and almonds. Montalcino stages a honey fair every September. Grosseto has been making its *pan ducale* bread since the Medici dukes gave it their blessing 400 years ago, but the recipe for its *torta etrusca* is shrouded in the mists of antiquity.

The wine towns also produce fine olive oils; Lucca proclaims its own oil to be the best.

For Chianti wines, the major buying centres apart from the vineyards themselves are Greve, Radda and Gaiole. Both Montepulciano and Montalcino consider their best vintages superior to anything Chianti can produce. For white wine, remember San Gimignano's Vernacchio, while Elba produces good sweet *Moscato* and *Aleatico* dessert wines. You might also like to consider the *grappa* brandies distilled in most of the wineries or the Camàldoli monks' liqueurs in the Casentino.

Dining Out

The key to the success of Italian cuisine has been straightforward treatment of fresh vegetables, fish and meat without elaborate heavy sauces. Italian cooks have travelled far afield to familiarize people everywhere with the classics of their national cuisine—from the pasta and pizza of Sicily and Naples in the south to the risotto and veal dishes of Venice, Bologna and Milan in the north. Between the two, Tuscany offers its own specialities, using the region's aromatic herbs and olive oil—best from Lucca—and perhaps less garlic than further south.

To start with...

One of the more attractive customs of a good trattoria is to display with an artistic flourish the multicoloured array of its *antipasti* (appetizers) on a buffet near the entrance. Besides the classic *peperoni*, red, green and yellow peppers marinated and grilled in olive oil and lemon juice, you will be offered an assortment, served cold, of baby marrows (*zucchini*), aubergines (*melanzane*), sliced fennel (*finocchio*), wild mushrooms (*funghi*), artichokes (*carciofi*). Seafood antipasti include fresh sardines (*sarde*), squid (*calamari*), baby octopus (*polpi*), scampi, prawns (*gamberi*), mussels (*cozze*).

Tuscan specialities include a salad of tuna fish with white beans and onions (*fagioli toscani e cipolle con tonno*). In Florence a variation of oven-roasted garlic-bread (*bruschetti*) is served with a topping of chopped chicken livers (*crostini di fegatini*), while San Gimignano's *crostini bianchi* uses cheese with white truffles, and the black version (*crostini neri*) anchovies and capers. Try the salami from Montepulciano, Siena and Arezzo—especially the *finocchiona* with fennel seeds, or peppery little sausages of wild boar meat (*salsiccioli secchi*).

Soups

Tuscany's distinctive *minestrone* uses celery and a little olive oil in place of northern Italy's Parmesan cheese. *Zuppa di fagioli e cavalo nero* is a lusty concoction of white beans and black cabbage spiced with garlic and parsley.

Pasta

Bowing to a more weight-wary clientèle, restaurants accept that people often want pasta as a main dish rather than the more traditional *primo piatto* (starter). Pasta noodles come in literally scores of different shapes, each appropriate to the sauce—tomato, vegetable, cheese, cream, fish or meat. Manufacturers even hire architects to design new variations on the corrugated *rigatoni*, quill-shaped *penne*, butterfly *farfalle*, curved *linguine* or flat *tagliatelle* and *pappardelle*. Among the classic sauces are minced meat *bolognese, pesto* (basil, garlic, pine nuts and Parmesan), *marinara* (shellfish), *vongole* (clams and tomato), *carbonara* (chopped bacon and eggs) and, simplest of all, *aglio e olio* (garlic and olive oil spiced with chilli peppers).

Tuscan specialities include pappardelle in an unctuous *lepre* sauce of hare in red wine; *cappelletti,* ravioli shaped like miniature hats; and spinach *gnocchi* (pasta of potato-flour or semolina). On your weekend in Umbria, sample Perugia's famous pasta *ai tartufi neri* (with black truffles). Incidentally, Perugia is known for its chocolate.

Fish

Seafood is more commonly served in coastal areas, grilled or fried with lemon—*triglia* (red

mullet), *spigola* (sea bass) or *pesce spada* (swordfish). Some local specialities: *sarde ripene* (fresh sardines stuffed with chopped egg, cheese, parsley and breadcrumbs); Pisa's *anguille in ginocchioni* (eel-stew); and *cacciucco*, Tuscany's answer to *bouillabaisse* (red mullet, crab and squid stewed in tomatoes, garlic, onion and Chianti).

Meat

Veal *(vitello)* remains popular, *tonnato* in tuna fish sauce or *alla fiorentina* in a spinach sauce. Other variations: *osso buco* (stewed veal shinbone), *scaloppine* (veal fillets), *costoletta* (pan-fried cutlet) and *saltimbocca* (small veal-rolls with ham, sage and Marsala wine). Tuscany claims to rear the country's best beef, actually *vitellone* "young beef" and served as *bistecca alla fiorentina*, a flat, thin, charcoal-grilled T-bone steak, as big as your plate. Free-range chicken is either grilled *(pollo alla diavola)* or pan-fried chicken breast *(petto di pollo alla fiorentina)*. Usually from September, wild game from the Casentino forests include *cervo con salsa di ciliege* (venison in cherry sauce), *lepre* (hare) and *cinghiale* (wild boar); for that Umbria trip, *palombacci alla perugina* (wood pigeons in a sauce of olives, juniper, sage and red wine).

Cheeses

Tuscany's ewe's milk cheese is particularly good in the *Crete* hills south of Siena—dry and tangy *pecorino* (also good in Pienza), creamy *raveggioli* and the well-known *ricotta* cottage-cheese.

Desserts

Save your craving for ice cream for a trip to the *gelateria*; the flavours are astounding. One local delicacy you might like to try is *budino toscano*, a Tuscan pudding of ricotta cheese, raisins, almonds, zests of orange and lemon and vanilla sugar.

Wines

You may like to compare the greater and lesser Chianti reds as well as the full bodied Montalcino and Montepulciano with their northern counterparts. Ask *quietly* for Piedmont's *Barolo*, *Barbera* or *Barbaresca* and your Tuscan wine-waiter may oblige, but he may give you a sour look if you ask for common-or-garden *Bardolino* or *Valpolicella* from around Verona and Lake Garda. The best of Tuscany's whites is the San Gimignano *Vernaccia*, which again can be compared with that of Umbria's Orvieto. Sweet dessert wines include Elba's *Moscato* and *Aleatico*, while all the best vineyards produce fine *Grappa* brandies.

Sports

Water sports on the Mediterranean may seem your best bet for time-off from sightseeing, but there are surprising alternatives.

Cycling

The hill-country of Tuscany may seem too gruelling for a casual bicycle excursion, but tours are arranged where you pedal from hotel to hotel while your luggage is carried by van. You could also consider it as a spectator-sport. The tough climbs and breath-taking downhill pursuits make the region ideal for cycle races. The killer Tour of Tuscany usually takes place in mid-May. And no Tour of Italy would be complete without routing a couple of stages through Tuscany some time from the end of May to June.

Watersports

For swimming, the best beaches are on Tuscany's north coast, at Viareggio and Forte dei Marmi, and further south at Punta Ala and Castiglione della Pescaia. On the island of Elba, the favourites are Marciana Marina and Biodola. (Pollution may be a problem on beaches around the ports of Piombino and Livorno.)

The seaside resorts all have rental facilities for diving, snorkelling, windsurfing, paragliding and water-skiing. The best sailing is at Argentario's Porto Ercole and Porto Santo Stefano.

Fishing

The Maremma coast around Talamone offers offshore spearfishing and angling. Freshwater fishing is possible in the upper Arno river in the Casentino. Ask the tourist office about a permit.

Hiking

The Tuscan hills are a hiker's paradise, but you should also consider exploring the cooler woodlands in the Maremma nature reserve or the Camàldoli forest in the Casentino. Poppi has an information centre for walking tours with good trail-maps.

Tennis and Golf

Resorts and some of the larger country hotels have tennis courts or can advise about the use of municipal courts.

There are dozens of wonderful golf courses in Tuscany. Full 18-hole courses are available at Punta Ala, Montecatini Terme and Grassina in Chianti.

The Hard Facts

Airports
Most regular international flights come into Galileo Galilei Airport at Pisa. A few European and domestic flights use Amerigo Vespucci Airport at Peretola, 5 km (3 miles) northwest of Florence. The terminals provide banking, car-hire and tourist information services, in additon to limited duty-free shopping, restaurant and snack bar facilities. There are taxis and airport buses to take you to major destinations.

Baggage
If you're travelling in the summer months, you'll need very little. In any case, clothing should be light; cottons are less sticky than synthetics. Unless you are going to a spa town like Montecatini Terme or another smart resort, you won't need much formal wear. Pack a sun-hat and add a sweater for cool evenings. Good walking shoes are vital. Include insect-repellent and a pocket torch.

Climate
Tuscany has a six-month summer, hot and dry from May to October. Temperatures in July and August are frequently over 30°C (86°F) and not much lower in June and September, but you can always cool off by the sea or up in the Casentino hills. The wine-harvest months of September and October can be very pleasant, with romantic mists in the valleys. Winters are generally cold and rainy, with surprisingly mild spells, especially on the coast. Many resort hotels close off-season.

Communications
If you want your mail to get home quickly, use the *Posta prioritaria* service, which works quite well (and put your postcards in an envelope). Italy now has a modern telecommunications system for fax and phone. Call worldwide with telecards from streetphones, much cheaper than the hotel's surcharge service. Remember that system of Italian phone-numbering demands the use of the 0 preceding the area code, even from abroad.

Crime
Pickpockets may be prevalent in crowded places in town and at the beach. Don't leave your handbag open or put your wallet in a hip pocket. Leave your valuables in the hotel safe. Lock your luggage before leaving it with porters at the airport.

Customs controls

Minimal at point of entry, with an official duty-free import allowance (subject to frequent change) of 200 cigarettes or 50 cigars or 250 g of tobacco, 1 litre of spirits 2 litres of still wine for visitors entering from countries outside the EU. If products and goods are bough tax-paid in an EU country, no restrictions are applied, as long as the goods are for personal use. No limit on amounts of foreign currency.

Driving

If renting a car, be sure to have a valid national licence or International Driving Permit. Rental age limit is usually over 21. Check on the exact extent of varying insurance coverages, personal, fire, collision, theft, etc. Speed limits are 50 kph in towns and 100 kph on the highway (90 kph on wet roads), 120 kph on the motorway (*autostrada*) (110 kph on wet roads). On some motorways with three lanes, 150 kph is allowed in dry weather.

Drive on the right, overtake on the left, even if you see impatient Italian drivers doing otherwise. Country roads in the hills may be occasionally bumpy, but the motorways run down the coast from Massa-Carrara to Livorno, and from Pisa across to the A1 Florence-Rome. Handle the separate Florence-Siena so-called *superstrada* with care. Petrol here is quite expensive and many filling stations close early on Saturday and all day Sunday.

Emergencies

Most problems can be handled at your hotel desk. Telephone number for police *(carabinieri)* is 112, fire brigade 115. Consular help is there only for critical situations, lost passports or worse, not for lost cash or plane tickets.

Formalities

A valid passport, or just an identity card for members of EC countries, is all most people need.

Health

Most health problems derive from too much sun or midday wine. Avoid excessive direct exposure to the sun. Wear a hat, use a sun-screen, and keep to the shady side of the street when sightseeing.

Residents of EU countries benefit from reciprocal health agreements. Before leaving home, ask at your post office for a form E111. Doctors, dentists and hospital staff are of good standard, many speaking some English.

Holidays and festivals

Tuscany's public holidays:

Jan 1	New Year
Jan 6	Epiphany
April 25	Liberation Day

May 1	Labour Day
Aug 15	Ferragosto: Assumption
Nov 1	All Saints' Day
Dec 8	Immaculate Conception
Dec 25–26	Christmas
Moveable	Easter Sunday and Monday

Religious (and pagan) festivals:

Feb	pre-Lenten Carnival, big in Viareggio
April 2	Lucca's costumed Liberty Festival, mass in cathedral
Easter	Prato holds festivities for the *Sacro Cingolo* (Holy Girdle)
May	Massa Marittima's *Girifalco* crossbow tournament
June 16	Pisa's Feast of San Ranieri
Late June	*Gioco di Ponte* tournament
July 2	Siena's *Palio*
Aug 16	Siena's *Palio*
Sept, 1st Sunday	Arezzo's *Giostra del Saracino* tournament.

Languages

Apart from Italian, the Tuscans use a dialect among themselves. At the resorts, hotel and restaurant staff speak some English, German or French.

Media

British and other European newspapers and overseas editions of the *International Herald Tribune* and *Wall Street Journal* arrive in Florence on the date of publication, but may take a day to reach outlying towns.

Many hotels have satellite reception for BBC, CNN and various European and North African channels.

If you are a short-wave enthusiast, find out from BBC World Service or Voice of America their current local wavelengths.

Money

The currency is the Euro, divided into 100 cents. Coins: 1, 2, 5, 10, 20 and 50 cents *(centesimi)*, 1 and 2 euros; banknotes: 5, 10, 20, 50, 100, 200 and 500 euros.

Shops and restaurants accept major credit cards and travellers cheques.

Opening hours

Banks generally open Monday to Friday 8.30 a.m. to 12.45 p.m. Most shops are open Monday to Saturday 8 a.m. to 1 p.m. and 3.30 p.m to 7.30 p.m.

Hours for most museums and historic sites may vary according to season and place, so it's best to check with the local tourist information office, but most close afternoons from 2 p.m. and all day Monday.

Public Transport

State railways *(FS: Ferrovie dello Stato)* link major towns, but the SITA buses are the best way to get around. Timetables can be obtained from the tourist office. The major problem may be making connections between the Florentine and Sienese networks.

Social graces

Tuscans are much more reserved than most other Italians. Their dignity is in fact quite refreshing and their hospitality unstinting once you have struck up an acquaintance. The year-round presence of tourists has accustomed them to boisterous behaviour. They shake hands but don't expect an affectionate Latin hug. They will be pleasantly surprised to hear you greet them with a couple of words of Italian. A *buon giorno* (good morning) or *buona sera* (good evening), *per piacere* (please), *grazie* (thanks) and *prego* (don't mention it) are always welcome. Remember to dress decently when entering a church.

Tipping

Service is included in restaurant and hotel bills, although an extra 5 or 10% is customary. Be careful when paying by credit card to fill in the "Total" line, often left blank for you to add, if you wish, an extra tip.

Toilets

The ladies' room is usually sign-posted *Signore,* and the men's by *Uomini.* If you are wary of public toilets, use the facilities in a bar or restaurant, but it is polite to order a drink beforehand.

Tourist Information Offices

Useful for museum opening hours, regional and city maps:

APT (Agenzia per il Turismo)
Via Manzoni 16, Florence
Tel. 055 233 20

Province and City of Florence
Via Cavour 1r
Tel. 055 290 832

City of Florence
Borgo Santa Croce 29
Tel. 055 234 04 44
Piazza della Stazione
Tel. 055 212 245

Siena
Piazza del Campo 56
Tel. 0577 280 551

Pisa
Via Nenni 24
Tel. 050 929 777

Arezzo
Piazza della Repubblica 28
Tel. 0575 377 678.

Voltage

Electric current is 220-volt 50-cycle AC, but take adaptors for any sensitive eletronic equipment like portable computers.

INDEX

GENERAL EDITOR
Barbara Ender-Jones
LAYOUT
Luc Malherbe
PHOTO CREDITS
All photos by A. Schroeder, except:
Hémisphères/Giraudou, pp. 72, 81, 84;
Hémisphères/Giulio, p. 75;
Hémisphères/Rieger, p. 76
MAPS
Elsner & Schichor

Copyright © 2003, 2001
by JPM Publications S.A.
12, avenue William-Fraisse,
1006 Lausanne, Switzerland
E-mail:
information@jpmguides.com
Web site:
http://www.jpmguides.com/

Printed in Switzerland
Weber/Bienne (CTP) – 03/04/01